Retroverting
Slavonic Pseudepigrapha

Society of Biblical Literature

Text-Critical Studies

Editor
James R. Adair, Jr.

Volume 3
RETROVERTING
SLAVONIC PSEUDEPIGRAPHA

Retroverting Slavonic Pseudepigrapha

Toward the Original of the Apocalypse of Abraham

Alexander Kulik

Society of Biblical Literature
Atlanta

Retroverting Slavonic Pseudepigrapha

Alexander Kulik

Copyright © 2004 by the Society of Biblical Literature

All rights reserved. No part of this work may be reproduced or transmitted in any form or by any means, electronic or mechanical, including photocopying and recording, or by means of any information storage or retrieval system, except as may be expressly permitted by the 1976 Copyright Act or in writing from the publisher. Requests for permission should be addressed in writing to the Rights and Permissions Office, Society of Biblical Literature, 825 Houston Mill Road, Atlanta, GA 30329, USA.

Library of Congress Cataloging-in-Publication Data

Kulik, Alexander.
  Retroverting Slavonic pseudepigrapha : toward the original of the Apocalypse of Abraham / by Alexander Kulik.
    p. cm. — (Text-critical studies ; no. 3)
  Includes bibliographical references.
  ISBN 1-58983-087-3 (pbk. : alk. paper)
  1. Apocalypse of Abraham—Criticism, Textual. I. Apocalypse of Abraham. English. II. Title. III. Series.

BS1830.A62K85 2004
229'.913—dc22

2004019374

08 07 06 05 04   5 4 3 2 1

Printed in the United States of America
on acid-free paper

To Lara

Table of Contents

Introduction 1

Apocalypse of Abraham: Translation 9

Chapter 1: Greek Vorlage 37
    Graphic misinterpretations 37
    Morphological calques 39
    Semantic calques 44
    Syntactic Hellenisms 55
    Phraseological Hellenisms 58

Chapter 2: Semitic Original 61
    Hebrew or Aramaic? 61
    May we retrovert the Hebrew original, omitting the Greek stage? ... 64
    Two-stage retroversion 66
        2.3.1. Semantic calques 66
        2.3.2. Syntactic biblicisms 69
        2.3.3. Phraseological biblicisms 71

Chapter 3: Textual Criticism and Retroversion 77

Chapter 4: Intertextual Verification as a Tool of Retroversion 81
    Biblical paraphrases 81
    Parallels from Pseudepigrapha 83
    Parallels from Jewish Hellenistic sources 84
    Parallels from Rabbinic sources 85
    Parallels from non-Jewish sources 88

Conclusions 91

Abbreviations 95
Manuscripts 97
References 99

Acknowledgements

I am grateful to my teachers and colleagues Moshe Altbauer ז״ל, Christian Hannick, James Kugel, Michael Stone, and especially to my dissertation adviser Moshe Taube, for their help and advice during the preparation of this work.

The research was conducted with the support of the Rotenstreich Foundation, the Memorial Foundation for Jewish Culture, and the Hebrew University Orion Center for the Study of the Dead Sea Scrolls and Associated Literature.

Introduction

Most early Slavonic documents are translated texts. Unlike Greek, Latin, and some other medieval sacral languages with developed pre-Christian literary traditions, Slavonic was initially created as a *lingua translationis* from Greek, and mainly from the "Semitized" Greek of the Bible and early Christian literature. Many of the Slavonic writings could hardly be properly interpreted without referring to their *Vorlage*. This problem is especially striking when we deal with those texts for which there are no surviving prototypes or versions in other languages.

The significance of some such texts goes far beyond their value for Slavic research, when their lost originals belong to ancient traditions that form the foundation of our culture. One of the most significant ancient documents to have been preserved solely in translation into Slavonic is the pseudepigraphon *Apocalypse of Abraham* (= *ApAb*).[1] Its lost Hebrew (or, less probably, Palestinian Aramaic) original may be defined as the earliest mystical writing of Judaeo-Christian civilization and as representative of a missing link between early apocalyptic and medieval *Hekhalot* traditions. *ApAb* is of great interest for the study of the roots of both rabbinic Judaism and early Christianity. At the same time, the Slavonic prototext of *ApAb* is no less important for the investigation of Slavonic literary activity at the very beginning of its development.

Contents

ApAb consists of two main parts—"aggadic" and "apocalyptic"— distinguished by genre and, according to some opinions, originally independent (see Ginzberg 1906:92). The two parts, nevertheless, make up a coherent narrative presenting a prehistory and expansion of the biblical story of Abraham's covenant with God (Gen 15). The first "aggadic" part (ch. 1–8) concerns Abraham's rejection of idolatry.[2] Having experienced the weakness of helplessly damaged idols (ch. 1–2), Abraham comes to the conclusion that idols are weaker than men, their makers (3:1–4), that they cannot help themselves

---

[1] On possible Arabic translation reflected in *Bulūqiyyā* see Wasserstrom 2000.
[2] Stories similar to the aggadic part are well attested in pseudepigrapha and especially in rabbinic sources; see *Jub* 12; *Gen. Rab.* 38:13; *Tanna debe Eliahu* 2:25; *Seder Eliahu Rabba* 33; cf. Horovits (1881:1,43–44); Jellinek (1853–1878:1.26;2.118–119); Margulies (1947:204–205).

(3:5–7), and therefore cannot help those who worship them (3:8). Trying to persuade his father Terah (ch. 4), Abraham performs a final test, this time intentional, of one of the idols (ch. 5). Then, pursuing the perfect object of worship, Abraham reflects on the hierarchy of idols (ch. 6) and then on the hierarchy of natural elements and luminaries (ch. 7:1–10). His reflection ends with a monotheistic conclusion (7:11–12). This leads to revelation and divine intervention which burns Terah's house but saves Abraham (ch. 8). The apocalyptic part, following this story, contains the descriptions of the "Covenant Between the Pieces" (ch. 9–14) and of the ascension to heaven, including the apocalypse itself (15–31).[3] The revelation, introduced already at the conclusion of the aggadic prehistory, continues with God's command on sacrifice (ch. 9; *ad* Gen 15:9). Abraham then receives instructions from the head of angels, Yahoel (ch. 10–11). They travel together to the prescribed place of the offering, mount Horeb (ch. 12), where Azazel tries to seduce Abraham (ch. 13–14; *ad* Gen 15:11). The fulfillment of the sacrifice is followed by the ascension to heaven (ch. 15), where Yahoel teaches Abraham a song praising God (ch. 16–17). In heaven Abraham sees the divine throne (ch. 18) and celestial "powers" on eight firmaments (ch. 19). The vision of the "lower" sky is followed by the "promise of seed" (20:1–5; *ad* Gen 15:5). The vision of earth contains figurative answers to two theological questions that Abraham raises. The first one has to do with the existence of evil in the world (20:7). It is answered by the vision of creation (21:1–22:2), inhabited by the chosen people and peoples belonging to Azazel, righteous and sinners (22:3–5), and by the vision of the first men seduced by Azazel (23:1–11). This leads Abraham to the second question: "why ... is evil desired in the heart of man?" (23:12–14). The answer, which contains allegorical depictions of the sins of heathens (ch. 24) and the sins of Israel (idolatry and murder, ch. 25; cf. 27:7), is concluded by the declaration of the principle of free will combined with predetermination (ch. 26). In the last chapters Abraham is shown the future of his progeny: the details of and the reasons for the destruction of the First Temple (ch. 27), the exile (28–29:3), the false and true Messiahs (29:4–14), the final judgment and salvation (29:14–21), the punishment of heathens and the gathering of Israel (ch. 30–31).

Original

The original of *ApAb* is presumed to have been composed in Palestine in the early centuries of the Common Era. It may be dated mainly on the basis of internal data (such as the relation of the document to the destruction of the Second Temple, etc.; cf. Kulik 1997b). The earliest reliable external evidence

---

[3] Parallels to the apocalyptic part, which are relevant for the puposes of retroversion, may be found below (see esp. ch. 4).

for the dating of *ApAb* is contained in the Clementine *Recognitiones* 32–33 (2nd cent.).[4] Both the contents and linguistic features of the document display its undoubtedly Jewish origin, while the specifically Essene milieu suggested by some scholars (see BL:21; Riesler 1928:1267) is not so obvious. The same is true of supposedly dualistic (ancient Gnostic or medieval Bogomil) and Christian interpolations and glosses (see, e.g., Frey 1928:31–32); some of these were recognized as such due to a misinterpretation of the text (see 20:5,7; 22:5; 29:3–13; cf. Licht 1971 and Hall 1988).

Extant Version

ApAb has come down to us in East Slavic copies dating from the 14th century onwards. In accordance with a very common pattern, these copies go back to the South Slavic prototext (translated from Greek), which, as Lunt (1985) has shown, may date to the 10th-11th centuries. A relatively full text of *ApAb* is found in six manuscripts from the 14th to 17th centuries, four of which are integrated into the *Palaea Interpretata* (mss ABCK; for abbreviations see the list of manuscripts). Other copies are obviously secondary and contain almost no independent evidence (cf. Lunt 1985:56 and n. 3; RL:686–687). *Codex Sylvester* (ms S) is the oldest and the only independent manuscript containing the full text of *ApAb*. Although it is also the most obscure and is considered "extremely faulty" (RL:686), abundant "in errors major and minor," it preserves valuable evidence of the Slavonic prototext and its sources. Important observations were also made on the basis of the readings in *Synodal Palaea* (Syn. 211, ms B). The detailed description and stratification of the manuscripts are presented by Turdeanu (1972), as well as in the critical editions by Philonenko (Phil:14–20) and Rubinkiewicz (Rub:15–27). See also brief but valuable characterizations in RL (681–682, 686–688) and Lunt (1985:55–56).

Scholarship

The history of the scholarship of *ApAb* involves more than a hundred years of largely fragmentary research abounding in translations based on incomplete evidence and short surveys based on these translations. The document was mentioned first in 1842 by Vostokov (Востоков 1842:728–734). A fragment of the oldest copy of *ApAb* preserved in *Codex Sylvester* (= S, 14th cent.) was published by Sreznevskij (Срезневский 1860:XX-XXI). There are three

---

[4] For a detailed discussion of the date of *ApAb*; see BL (XV-XIX); Phil (34–35); RL (683); Rub (70–73); Kulik (1997b); cf. our comm. to 1:9; 9:9; 27:5.

editions of the complete text of S: by Sreznevskij (Срезневский 1861–1863:648–665), Tikhonravov (1863:32–78—together with the text from *Volokolamsk Palaea* = A, 15th cent.) and Novitskij (Новицкий 1891, facsimile edition). Porfir'ev published a copy dating from the 16th-17th cents. (*Solovetsk Palaea* = K). The facsimile edition of the version from the 16th-cent. *Synodal Palaea* (= B) was included in the critical edition by Rubinkiewicz of 1987 (Rub:227–257). Some fragments were also published by Pypin (Пыпин 1862:2.24–26) and Franko (Франко 1896:80–84). In 1897 *ApAb* was translated into German by Bonwetsch (Bonw). This translation contained an apparatus based on four manuscripts. Another German translation was accomplished by Riesler in 1928. In 1918 Box and Landsman published an English translation accompanied by a detailed commentary and introduction (BL). Since then, *ApAb* has been translated into English twice: by Rubinkiewicz in 1983 (RL; noted by Lunt) and by Pennington in 1985. French translations were included in the critical editions by both Philonenko (Phil) and Rubinkiewicz (Rub). Among the most significant articles the following should be mentioned: Frey (1928), Ginzberg (1906), Licht (1971), Rubinkiewicz (1974; 1979; 1980), and Rubinstein (1953; 1954; 1957). See also Hall (1984), Weitzman (1994), and Kulik (1997a,b). The article by Turdeanu (1972), which laid the basis for critical editions of the document, and the important work by Lunt (1985) on the language of *ApAb* deserve special attention. Our study is possible thanks to the publications of critical editions by Philonenko-Sayar and Philonenko in 1981 (Phil) and by Rubinkiewicz in 1987 (Rub). We recommend to use these editions during the examination of the present work. A more detailed up-to-date bibliography on the issue may be found in Kulik 2002.

Purposes and Methods

Our goal is to take a further step in the research on *ApAb*. The extraordinary obscurity of the text of *ApAb* cannot be explained only by corruption in the process of inner-Slavonic transmission of the document. We assume that a significant part of the problems of interpretation go back to an early and sometimes very literal translation. It is well known that "the main reason for incomprehensibility [of early Slavonic texts] is, of course, literal translation, and the list of works in which whole passages are completely without meaning in Slavonic is long …" (Thomson 1978:117). As we shall see below, our text has some features of those sacral *verbum de verbo* translations which were created as "rewriting of the original with corresponding lexical items from the receptor language" (Nida 1964:186; cf. Thomson 1988b). Thus, the only way to improve our understanding of the document is to retrovert fragments of its Greek *Vorlage* and, sometimes, even of the Semitic original.

The absence of a developed general methodology of retroversion (which, moreover, must differ for different cultural patterns) deprives us of the advantage of an a priori methodological approach. The elaboration of principles and tools for the retroversion based on Slavonic material should be preceded by practical application to a wide range of texts and the accumulation of successful solutions. Our exercise belongs to the first stage of this accumulation, in which we deal with separate problems of interpretation, trying to solve them by means of retroversion. In other words, we see ourselves methodologically committed to a convincing retroversion of any obscure or ambiguous portion of the text, until we are assured that its difficulty does not originate from the stage of translation.

This purpose must include two overlapping tasks: (1) to characterize a lost text on the basis of a secondary translation thereof and (2) to improve the interpretation of a preserved text on the basis of a reconstruction of its lost sources. Thus, the results of such study will be of two types: innovative linguistic interpretations and textual choices based on retroversions on the one hand, and reconstructed Greek and Semitic forms presenting the evidence for a lost Greek *Vorlage* and Semitic original on the other. Hence, almost every comment in this interdisciplinary study can be elaborated from the points of view of its contribution both to Slavic philology and to Jewish studies (for examples of the former see Kulik 1997a, and of the latter, Kulik 1997b). However, we limit ourselves here to bringing together the primary data necessary to generate innovative interpretations and to provide a sufficient basis for independent research in each of these disciplines.

Most of the retroversions become possible when the translation either cites (paraphrases) a known text or imitates the linguistic structure of the *Vorlage*. This imitation results mainly from either misinterpretation or a tendency to literalism: "the more literal the translation, the more reliable the retroversion" (Olofsson 1990:73; cf. Tov 1981:101). The main criteria of our retroversions are the linguistic demands of the target languages and the contextual probability, examined, when possible, against the intertextual background, including precedents on the level of translation or parallels on the level of *Vorlage* and original. The Slavonic Bible, thus, is very useful for our purpose, since it passed the same stages of transmission as *ApAb* (Hebrew/Aramaic- Greek-Slavonic), but in contrast to *ApAb*, its Greek *Vorlage* and Semitic original have survived as LXX and MT. Lexical equivalents from these three sources (or groups of sources) are well reflected in lexicography (see below, *Structure*). This is one of the reasons for the fact that more space in this work is allotted to lexica than to morphology or syntax. We may also plead in excuse that the tools for lexical reconstruction are incomparably better elaborated: here we can base ourselves on typology, precedents from other translations, and not only on speculations based on single cases. As noted in regard to the reconstruction of the Hebrew *Vorlage* of LXX, "a retroversion on the semantic level based on a study of translation technique that concerns the vocabulary of the translators can be made with a reasonable degree of certainty," while grammatical deviations "cannot be reconstructed with confidence" (Olofsson 1990:71; cf. Tov 1981:100–101, 114; Barr 1968:265–266).

Structure

This study is organized formally as a discussion of separate problematic segments of the text, classified according to the types of the retroverted phenomena. We proceed from the problems of the retroversion of the Greek *Vorlage* (chapter 1) to the cases where the reconstruction of the Semitic original is involved (chapter 2). These chapters are followed by the examination of the cases where retroversion is interlaced with text-critical problems (chapter 3) and intertextual analysis (chapter 4). The classification and arrangement of cases to different chapters is sometimes impeded by the fact that one case may involve more than one type of analysis. For this reason all chapters have cross-references. The Slavonic text of the passages discussed, with indications of all significant discrepancies, is cited in standard transliteration used also in both editions of *ApAb* (*e* for к, *o* for w, *y* for оү and ѫ, *ю* for ѭ, *я* for ꙗ, ѧ, ѩ). The texts and apparatuses of the editions (Phil and Rub) are used critically and are checked against the manuscripts at our disposal. We strongly recommend to use *both* critical editions of *ApAb* (Phil and Rub) while examining this study. The justification of reconstructions may not be presented in cases of widespread regular equivalents well attested in lexicography (mainly by Slov, Mikl, Srezn, SRJa11–17 and SDRJa11–14 for Greek-Slavonic "formal equivalents" and HR for Hebrew/Aramaic-Greek ones attested in LXX and οἱ γ´).

Translation

The work is prefaced by a translation of the entire document. It presents the context of the fragments discussed in the study and thus serves two main purposes: (1) to illustrate the contextual considerations of new interpretations and (2) to reflect the interpretive innovations and their influence on the understanding of the broader text. The translation functions also as a basis for cross-references. We have taken into account the achievements of previous English translations, while, as stated above, basing ourselves on new readings developed in the present study. Words added in order to clarify a literal translation are put in square brackets "[ ]." Although the translation is not accompanied by an apparatus, the elements of the text which do not occur in the version of the *Codex Sylvester* (ms S) are enclosed in triangular brackets "< >"; this is justified by the significant divergence of this oldest manuscript from other versions. Semitic proper names are presented in their reconstructed original forms: this holds for common biblical names, such as Abraham, Terah, or Michael, as well as for the names which are unique to this document, such as Mar-Umath(a) (CS *Marumafa* and *Marumat*, Gk *Marumatha/Marumat*), Bar-Eshath(a) (CS and Middle Gk *Varisat*), rare Azazel (CS and Middle Gk *Azazil*), or Ya(h)oel (CS and Middle Gk *Iaoil*), which occurs also in the Slavonic *Life of Adam and Eve*. We follow the chapter division established by Bonwetsch (Bonw) and the verse division of RL (with exceptions conditioned by new syntactic divisions).

Translation

i. Prehistory: Abraham The Iconoclast (1–8)

i.i. Abraham Tests Idols (1–2)

i.i.i. Fall of Mar-Umath (1)

1:1 On the day when I was destroying[1] the gods of my father Terah and the gods of my brother Nahor, when I was testing which one was the truly strong god,

1:2 at the time when my lot came up, when I had finished the services of my father Terah's sacrifice to his gods of wood, stone, gold, silver, brass and iron,

1:3 I, Abraham, having entered their temple for the service,[2] found a god named Mar-Umath,[3] carved out of stone, fallen at the feet of an iron god, Nakhon.[4]

1:4 And it came to pass, that when I saw this, my heart was troubled. And I fell to thinking, because I, Abraham, was unable to return him to his place all by myself, since he was heavier than[5] a great stone.

1:5 And I went and told my father. And he entered with me.

1:6 And as we both were moving him [Mar-Umath] to return him in his place, his head fell off of him, while I was still holding him by his head.

1:7 And it came to pass, when my father saw that the head of Mar-Umath had fallen off of him, he said to me, "Abraham!"

1:8 And I said, "Here am I!" And he said to me, "Bring me an axe and a chisel[6] from the house."

For the principles and conventions of the translations see Introduction. The footnotes to the translation contain references to the sections discussing the marked verses.

[1] CS *настрьзати*—Gk ἐπικείρω 'destroy' or ἐπιξέω/ἐπιξύω 'carve' (see 1.2.1).

[2] CS *службы требы*—Gk λειτουργίαι θυσίας—Heb עבודות הקרבן (see 4.4.1).

[3] CS *Марумафъ*—Aram (א)מר אומת "the lord of the nation" (see 2.1.1).

[4] CS *Нахон*—Heb נכון 'stable; firmly established' (see 2.1.3).

[5] CS *отъ*—Gk ἐκ —Heb/Aram מ-, here 'than' (see 2.3.1.1).

[6] CS **измалъ*—Gk *ιζμαλ(ος)—Heb אזמל (see 2.2.1).

1:9 And I brought [them] to him from the house. And he carved[7] another Mar-Umath, out of another stone, without a head, and [placed on him] the head that had been thrown down from Mar-Umath, and smashed the rest of Mar-Umath.[8]

i.i.ii. Fall of Five Idols (2)

2:1 And he made five other gods, and he gave them to me [and] told me to sell them outside in the street of the town.[9]

2:2 And I saddled my father's ass and put them on it [and] went out to the main road to sell them.

2:3 And behold, merchants from Paddan Aram came with camels to go to Egypt to buy <kokonil[10] from the Nile there.

2:4 And I greeted them and they answered me>.[11] And I began to talk with them. One of their camels bellowed. The ass took fright and he ran and threw down the gods. And three of them were smashed and two remained.

2:5 And it came to pass, when the Syrians saw that I had gods, they said to me,

> "Why did you not tell us that <you had gods?
> We would have bought them> before the ass heard the camel's cry
> and you would have had no loss.

2:6 Give <us> at least the remaining gods
and we will give you a proper price."

2:7 <And I thought [it over] in my heart. And they gave [also] the price> of the smashed gods for the gods that remained.

2:8 Since I had been distressed in my heart [wondering], "How would I let my father know about the matter?!"[12]

2:9 And the debris of the smashed [gods] I cast into the water of the river Gur, which was at that place. And they sank into the depths and were no more.

---

[7] CS усѣчи—Gk πελεκάω 'hew' taken for πελεκίζω 'behead' (1.1.2).
[8] See 2.1.1.
[9] CS внѣ на пути градьсцѣмъ (S градьстѣмъ al.)—Gk ἔξω ἐν τῇ ὁδῷ τῆς πόλεως—Heb בחוץ ברחובה של העיר (see 4.1.2).
[10] CS коконилъ—Gk κόκκον Νείλου (see 1.1.1).
[11] The portions of text which do not occur in the version of *Codex Sylvester* (ms S) are enclosed in triangular brackets.
[12] CS принести куплю—Gk παρέχειν πρᾶγμα τινί "to cause trouble to s.-o." or Gk <?>—Heb הביא דבר אל "let s.-o. know about the matter" (see 2.3.3.1).

i.ii. Abraham Reflects on Idolatry (3)

3:1   And while I was still walking on the road, my heart was disturbed and my mind was distracted. And I said in my heart,

3:2   <"What is the profit of the labor which my father is doing?[13]
3:3   Is not he rather a god of his gods,
since by his sculpting, carving and skill they come into being?
3:4   It would be more fitting for them to worship my father,
since they are his work.
What gain is there for my father in his own works?>
3:5   Behold, Mar-Umath[14] fell
and was unable to get up again in his own temple,
nor could I lift him on my own,
until my father came and we both lifted him.
3:6   And as we were unable, his head fell off of him.
And he placed it on another stone of another god,
which he had made without a head.
3:7   And [likewise were] the other five gods
which were smashed down from the ass,
which were able neither to save themselves
nor to hurt the ass for it smashed them,
nor did their shards come up from the river."

3:8   And I said to myself,[15] "If it is thus, how then can my father's god, Mar-Umath, having a head of one stone and [the rest] being made of another stone, save a man, or hear a man's prayer and reward him?"

i.iii. Abraham Preaches Monotheism (4–8)

i.iii.i. Attempt to Persuade Terah (4)

4:1   And thinking thus, I came to my father's house and watered the ass and set out hay for it. I brought out the money and gave it into the hand of my father Terah.
4:2   When he saw it, he was glad, and he said,

---

[13] CS что си лихоть дѣяния еже дѣеть отьць мои—Gk τίς περίσσεια ἐν τῷ μόχθῳ ᾧ μοχθεῖ πατήρ μου—Heb מה יתרון בעמלו שיעמל אבי (see 4.1.1).
[14] See 2.1.1.
[15] CS и рѣкохъ къ срьдцу моему—Heb ואומר אל לבי (see 2.1.4).

	"Blessed by my gods are you, Abraham,[16]
	for you gave honor to the gods,[17]
	so that my labor was not in vain!"

4:3   And I declared and said to him,

"Hear, Terah, [my] father!
It is the gods who are blessed by <you,
since you are a god to them,
since you> have made them;
since their blessing is perdition, and their power is vain.

4:4   They could not help themselves,
how [then] will they help you or bless me?

4:5   [In fact] I was for you a kind god of this gain,
since it was through my cleverness that I brought you the money
for the smashed [gods]."

4:6   And when he heard my word, his anger was kindled against me, since I had spoken harsh words against his gods.

i.iii.ii. Fall of Bar-Eshath (5)

5:1   When I saw[18] my father's anger, I went out. <And afterward, when I had gone out,> he called me, saying, "Abraham!"

5:2   And I said, "Here am I!"

5:3   And he said, "Gather and take the splinters from the wood out of which I was making wooden gods before you came [and] cook me a meal!"

5:4   And it came to pass, when I was collecting the wooden splinters, I found among them a small god, lying among the pieces of wood on my left.

5:5   And on his forehead was written: "god Bar-Eshath."[19]

5:6   <And it came to pass, when I found him, I held back> and did not tell my father that I had found the wooden god Bar-Eshath among the chips. And it came to pass, after I had put the splinters on the fire, in order to cook food for my father, that I went out to ask about the food and I put Bar-Eshath near the hearth of fire, saying to him menacingly,

---

[16] CS блг҃слвнъ ты аврааме бм҃ъ моимъ—Gk εὐλογημένος (or: εὐλογητός) σου Ἀβραμ τοῖς θεοῖς μου—Heb ברוך אתה אברם לאלהי (see 2.3.2.1).

[17] CS принести цѣну "bring a price"—Gk τιμὴν φέρειν "give an honor" (see 1.5.1).

[18] CS прѣмыслити—Gk κατανοέω—Heb ראה, צפה (see 1.2.2).

[19] CS Варисатъ—Gk *Βαρησατ/θ(α)—Aram בר אשת(א) 'fiery' (see 2.1.2).

Translation

5:7 "Bar-Eshath, make sure that the fire does not go out before I come back. If the fire does go out, blow on it to make it flare up."

5:8 [And] I went out, having kindled my fire.[20]

5:9 When I came back again I found Bar-Eshath fallen backwards, his feet enveloped in fire and terribly burned.

5:10 Laughing greatly to myself, I said, "Bar-Eshath, you certainly are able to kindle fire and cook food!"

5:11 And it came to pass, while I was speaking laughingly, that he was gradually[21] burned up by the fire and became ashes.

5:12 And I brought the food to my father, [and] he ate.

5:13 And I gave him wine and milk, and he drank and satiated himself and blessed Mar-Umath, his god.

5:14 And I said to him, "Father Terah, do not bless your god Mar-Umath, do not praise him! Praise rather your god Bar-Eshath because, in his love for you he threw himself into the fire in order to cook your food."

5:15 And he said to me, "And where is he now?"

5:16 "He has been reduced to ashes in the fury of the fire and become dust."

5:17 And he said,

> "Great is the power of Bar-Eshath!
> I shall make another today,
> and tomorrow he will make my food!"

i.iii.iii. Hierarchy of Gods (6)

6:1 When I, Abraham, heard such words from my father, I [both] laughed in my mind and [yet] groaned in the bitterness <and> anger of my soul.[22]

6:2 And I said, "How can a statue made by my father [ever] be his helper?

6:3 Or would he have subordinated his body to his soul, his soul to his spirit, then his spirit—to folly and ignorance?"[23]

6:4 And I said, "Must one put up with evil? Let me risk my life[24] for purity and I shall put forth my own clear thinking before him!"

6:5 I declared and said,

---

[20] CS *сътворити свѣтъ*—Gk φῶς ποιεῖν (see 1.5.2).

[21] CS *помалу помалу* (ms B)—Gk κατὰ μικρὸν μικρόν—Heb מעט מעט (see 3.1).

[22] CS *в горести… душа своея*—Heb במר נפשי (see 2.3.3.2).

[23] CS *или убо тѣло повинулъ будетъ своеи дши и дшю дхови а дха безумью и невѣжествию*—Heb שעבד את נפשו לרוחו ורוח להוללות ושכלות (see 4.3.2).

[24] CS *вергу умъ свои*—Gk ῥίψω τὴν ψυχήν μου—Heb אשלך נפשי (see 2.3.3.3).

	"Father Terah, whichever of these gods you praise, you err in your thinking.
6:6	Behold, my brother Nahor's gods standing in the holy temple are more honored than yours.
6:7	For behold, Zoukh,[25] my brother Nahor's god, is more honored than your god Mar-Umath, since he is made of gold sold by men.
6:8	And if he becomes worn out with the years, he will be remade, whereas Mar-Umath,[26] if he is changed or broken, will not be remade, since he is of stone.
6:9	[And] what about Yoavon,[27] a god <who is in the power of another god>, who stands beside Zoukh? <Since [even] he is more honored than the god Bar-Eshath[28] who is made of wood, while [Yoavon is] forged of silver. And being better proportioned,[29] he is sold by men in order to show him.>
6:10	But Bar-Eshath <, your god, before he was made had been rooted in the ground.
6:11	Being great and wondrous, with branches, flowers and [various] beauties.
6:12	And you cut him with an ax, and by your skill the god was made.
6:13	And behold, he has dried up, and his sap is gone.
6:14	He fell from the heights to the ground, and he went from greatness to insignificance,
6:15	and his appearance[30] has faded.>
6:16	[Now] he himself has been burned up by the fire,
6:17	and he turned into ashes and is no more.
6:18	Yet you say: "Today I shall make another one, and tomorrow he will make my food."
6:19	[But] he retained no strength[31] utterly perishing!

i.iii.iv. Hierarchy of Natural Elements and Luminaries (7)

7:1	This I say:

---

[25] CS *Зоухъ/Зоухе/Зоухии*—cf. Gk Ζουχ/Ζουχε/*Ζουχιος (see 4.5).
[26] See 2.1.1.
[27] CS *Иоавонъ*—cf. Gk Ιαβω, Ιαβου, Ιαου (see 4.5).
[28] See 2.1.2.
[29] CS *съпримѣрение* (< *съпримѣренѣе*)—Gk συμμετρότερος (see 1.2.3).
[30] CS *взоръ лица его*—Gk ὁ ὄψις τοῦ προσώπου αὐτου—Heb דמות פניו (see 2.3.3.4).
[31] CS *ни силы остави*—Gk καὶ οὐκ ἐκράτησα ἰσχύος—Heb ולא עצר כח or ולא נשאר בו כח (see 2.3.3.5).

7:2	Fire is the noblest [element] in the image [of the world], since even the things which are [otherwise] unsubdued are subdued in it, and [since] it mocks with its flames the things which perish easily.
7:3	<But I would not call it a god either, since it is subjugated to water.>
7:4	Water is indeed nobler, since it overcomes fire and soaks the earth.
7:5	But I would not call it a god, since it is subjugated to the earth, running underneath it.
7:6	I would rather call the earth the noblest, since it overcomes the substance and abundance of water.
7:7	But neither would I call it gods, since it is dried up by the sun [and since it is] made for men to plow.[32]
7:8	<[So] I would call the sun nobler than the earth,> since with its rays it illumines the inhabited world and the various airs.
7:9	But I would not make it into a god[33] either, since its course is obscured [both] at night [and] by the clouds.
7:10	Nor, again, would I call the moon and the stars gods, since they too in their times at night can darken their light.

i.iii.v. Monotheistic Conclusion (7:11–12)

7:11	Listen, Terah, my father, I shall seek in your presence the God[34] who created all the gods which we consider!
7:12	For who is it, or which one is it who colored[35] heaven and made the sun golden, who has given light to the moon and the stars with it, who has dried the earth in the midst of many waters, who set you yourself among the elements, and who now has chosen me in the distraction of my mind?— Will he reveal himself by himself to us?— [He is] the God!"

---

[32] CS дѣло from Gk ἐργάζωμαι—Heb עבד here 'plow' (see 1.3.2).

[33] CS того въ бг положу—Heb אשימנו לאלהים (see 2.3.3.6).

[34] CS възищу (SUD възвѣщу al.) предъ тобою бога—Heb (הים)אדרש את/אל/ל/ב אל (see 3.2).

[35] CS убагрити—Gk πορφύρω (see 1.3.3).

i.iii.vi. Punishment of Terah (8)

8:1 And as I was thinking about these things, here is what happened to my father Terah in the courtyard of his house: The voice of the Mighty One came down from heaven in a stream of fire, saying and calling, "Abraham, Abraham!"
8:2 And I said, "Here am I!"
8:3 And he said,

> "In the wisdom of your heart you are searching for the God of gods and the Creator.
> I am he!

8:4 Leave Terah your father, and leave the house, so that you too are not slain for the sins of your father's house!"

8:5 And I went out. And it came to pass as I was going out, that I had not even gotten as far as going beyond the doors of the courtyard
8:6 when the sound of thunder came forth and burned him and his house and everything in the house, down to the ground [to a distance of] forty cubits.

ii. Revelation (9–32)

ii.i. Sacrifice (9–14)

ii.i.i. Command on Sacrifice (9)

9:1 Then came a voice saying to me twice, "Abraham, Abraham!"
9:2 And I said "Here am I!"
9:3 And he said,

> "Behold, it is I!
> Fear not, for I am the primordial[36] and mighty God,
> who initially created the two luminaries[37] of the world.

9:4 I protect you[38] and I am your helper.

---

[36] CS *прежде вѣка*—Gk πρὸ τῶν αἰώνων, or Gk ἕως εἰς τὸν αἰῶνα—Heb עד עולם here 'for ever' (see 1.3.4.).

[37] CS *свѣта* dual. 'lights'—Gk φῶτα here dual: 'luminaries'—Heb אורות(מ) (see 1.3.5).

9:5	Go, take for me a heifer in her third year, and a she-goat in her third year, and ram in his third year, and a turtledove, and a pigeon, and set out for me a pure sacrifice.
9:6	And in this sacrifice I shall set before you the ages and make you know secrets,[39] and you will see great things which you have not seen, since you loved to search for me, and I called you 'my friend.'
9:7	But for forty days abstain from every food which issues from fire, and from the drinking of wine, and from anointing [yourself] with oil.
9:8	And then you shall set out for me the sacrifice which I have commanded you, in the place which I shall show you on a high mountain.
9:9	And there shall I show you the ages: things built and firmed, made and renewed[40] by my word.
9:10	And I shall make you know what will come to pass in them on those who have done evil and [those who have done] just things among the race of men."

ii.i.ii. Angel Yahoel (10–11)

10:1	And it came to pass, when I heard the voice announcing such words to me, and I looked hither and thither.
10:2	And behold, there was no breath of man, and my spirit was affrighted, and my soul fled from me,[41] and I became like a stone, and fell down upon the earth, for there was no longer strength in me to stand up on the earth.
10:3	And when I was still face down on the earth, I heard the voice <of the Holy One>, saying, "Go, Yahoel, the namesake[42] of the mediation of my ineffable name, sanctify this man and strengthen him from his trembling!"
10:4	And the angel whom he sent to me in the likeness of a man came, and he took me by my right hand and stood me on my feet.
10:5	And he said to me,

---

[38] CS *азъ есмь о тебѣ щитя*—Heb אנכי מגן עליך (see 2.2.3).

[39] CS *съблюденая*—Heb נצורות (see 4.4.2).

[40] Ms S has CS *поновения*—possibly Gk ἐγκαίνια—Heb חנוכה (see 1.3.6).

[41] CS *ужасе ся дхъ мои и избѣже дша моя отъ мене*—Gk ἡ πνεῦμα μου ἐταράχθη καὶ ψυχή μου ἐξῆλθεν—Heb נבהלה רוחי ונפשי יצאה ממני (see 4.1.3).

[42] CS *тьзъ* + gen.—Gk ἐπώνυμος + gen. "name-sake of" (see 1.4.1).

	"Stand up, <Abraham,> the friend of God who has loved you,
	let human trembling not enfold you.
10:6	For behold, I am sent to you to strengthen you and to bless you in the name of God,
	the creator of heavenly and earthly things, who has loved you.
10:7	Be bold and hasten to him.
10:8	I am Yahoel named by him
	who shakes those which are with me on the seventh vault, on the firmament.
	I am a power in the midst of the Ineffable
	who put together his names in me.
10:9	I am appointed according to his commandment
	to reconcile the rivalries of the Living Creatures of the Cherubim against one another, and teach those who bear him [to sing] the Song in the middle of man's night, at the seventh hour.
10:10	I am made in order to rule over the Leviathans,
	since the attack and the threat of every reptile are subjugated to me.
10:11	<I am ordered to unlock Hades and to destroy those who worship the dead things.>
10:12	I am ordered to burn your father's house with him, for he honored the dead things.
10:13	I am sent to you now to bless you and the land which the Eternal One, called by you, has prepared for you.
10:14	And for your sake I have indicated the way of earth.[43]
10:15	Stand up, Abraham, go boldly, be very joyful and rejoice!
	And I am with you,
	since an honorable portion has been prepared for you by the Eternal One.
10:16	Go, fulfill your sacrifice of the command!
	For behold, I am appointed to be with you and with the progeny which is due to be born from you.
10:17	And Michael is with me in order to bless you forever.
	Be bold, go!"

ii.i.iii. Journey to Horeb (12)

11:1   And I stood and saw him who had taken my right hand and set me on my feet.

---

[43] CS *путь земныи*—Heb ארח עולם/דרך ארץ (see 2.2.4).

11:2	The appearance of the griffin's body[44] was like sapphire, and the likeness of his face like chrysolite, and the hair of his head like snow,
11:3	and a turban on his head like the appearance of the bow in the clouds, and the closing of his garments [like] purple, and a golden staff [was] in his right hand.
11:4	And he said to me "Abraham!" and I said, "Here is your servant!" And he said,

> "Let my appearance not frighten you,
> nor my speech trouble your soul!

11:5	Come with me and I shall go with you,

> visible until the sacrifice, but after the sacrifice invisible forever.

11:6	Be bold and go!"
12:1	And we went, the two of us alone together, forty days and nights.
12:2	And I ate no bread and drank no water, because [my] food was to see the angel who was with me, and his speech with me was my drink.
12:3	And we came to the glorious God's mountains—Horeb.
12:4	And I said to the angel, "Singer of the Eternal One, behold, I have no sacrifice with me, nor do I know a place for an altar on the mountain, so how shall I make the sacrifice?"
12:5	And he said, "Look behind you."
12:6	And I looked behind me. And behold, all the prescribed sacrifices were following us: the calf, the she-goat, the ram, the turtledove, and the pigeon.
12:7	And the angel said to me, "Abraham!" And I said, "Here am I!"
12:8	And he said to me, "Slaughter and cut all this, putting together the two halves, one against the other. But do not cut the birds.
12:9	And give them [halves] to the two men whom I shall show you standing beside you, since they are the altar on the mountain, to offer sacrifice to the Eternal One.
12:10	The turtledove and the pigeon you will give me, and I shall ascend in order to show to you [the inhabited world] on the wings of two birds, in heaven and on the earth:

> the sea, and the abysses,
> and the depths, and the garden of Eden,
> and its rivers and the fullness of the inhabited world
> and round about it you will see[45] everything."

---

[44] See 4.2.
[45] CS *узрѣти въ*—Heb/Aram -ב ראה/חזי (see 2.3.2.3).

ii.i.iv. Azazel (13–14)

13:1 And I did everything according to the angel's command. And I gave to the angels who had come to us the divided parts of the animals. And the angel took the two birds.

13:2 And I waited for [the time of] the evening offering.[46]

13:3 And an impure bird flew down on the carcasses, and I drove it away.

13:4 And the impure bird spoke to me and said, "What are you doing, Abraham, on the holy heights, where no one eats or drinks, nor is there upon them food of men. But these will all be consumed by fire and they will burn you up.

13:5 Leave the man who is with you and flee! Since if you ascend to the height, they will destroy you."

13:6 And it came to pass when I saw the bird speaking I said to the angel, "What is this, my lord?" And he said, "This is iniquity, this is Azazel!"

13:7 And he said to him,

"Reproach is on you, Azazel!
Since Abraham's portion is in heaven, and yours is on earth,

13:8 Since you have chosen it and desired it to be the dwelling place of your impurity. Therefore the Eternal Lord, the Mighty One, has made you a dweller on earth.[47]

13:9 And because of you [there is] the wholly-evil spirit of the lie,
and because of you [there are] wrath and trials on the generations of impious men.

13:10 Since the Eternal Mighty God did not send the righteous, in their bodies, to be in your hand,
in order to affirm through them the righteous life and the destruction of impiety.

13:11 Hear, adviser! Be shamed by me,
since you have been appointed to tempt not to all the righteous!

13:12 Depart from this man!

13:13 You cannot deceive him, because he is the enemy of you
and of those who follow you and who love what you desire.

13:14 For behold, the garment which in heaven was formerly yours has been set aside for him,
and the corruption which was on him has gone over to you."

---

[46] CS *даръ вечерьнии*—Gk *) δῶρον ἑσπερινόν—Heb מנחת (ה)ערב (see 2.2.2).

[47] CS *дасть тя прѣвечный владыка крѣпкый житель на земли*—Heb נתנך ה' אל גיבור תושב/גר על הארץ (see 2.3.2.2).

14:1	And the angel said to me, <"Abraham!" And I said, "Here am I, your servant."
14:2	And he said, "Know by this that the Eternal One whom you have loved has chosen you.
14:3	Be bold and have power,⁴⁸ as I order you, over him who reviles justice,
14:4	or else I shall not be able to revile him who scattered about the earth the secrets of heaven and who conspired against the Mighty One>.
14:5	Say to him,

> 'May you be the fire brand of the furnace of the earth!
> Go, Azazel, into the untrodden parts of the earth.

14:6	<Since your inheritance are those who are with you, with men born with the stars and clouds. And their portion is you, and they come into being through your being.
14:7	And justice is your enmity. Therefore through your own destruction vanish from before me!'"
14:8	And I said the words as the angel had taught me.
14:9	And he said, "Abraham!" And I said, "Here am I, your servant!">
14:10	And the angel said to me, "Answer him not!"
14:11	<And he spoke to me a second time.
14:12	And the angel said, "Now, whatever he says to you, answer him not, lest his will affect you.>
14:13	Since God gave him <the gravity and> the will against those who answer him. <Answer him not."
14:14	And I did what the angel had commanded me.> And whatever he said to me about the descent, I answered him not.

ii.ii. On Heaven (15–31)

ii.ii.i. Ascension (15–16)

15:1	And it came to pass that when the sun was setting, and behold, a smoke like that of a furnace, and the angels who had the divided parts of the sacrifice ascended from the top of the furnace of smoke.

---

⁴⁸ CS *творити власть* + *на* + acc. Gk ἐξουσιάζω + ἐπί + acc. 'have power over s.-o.' (see 1.4.2).

15:2	And the angel took me with his right hand and set me on the right wing of the pigeon and he himself sat on the left wing of the turtledove, since they both were neither slaughtered nor divided.
15:3	And he carried me up to the edge of the fiery flame.
15:4	And we ascended <like great winds to the heaven which was fixed on the expanses.
15:5	And I saw on the sky,> on the height <we had ascended,> a strong light which cannot be described.
15:6	And behold, in this light a fire was kindled [and there was] of a crowd of many people[49] in male likeness.
15:7	They were all changing in appearance and likeness, running and being transformed and bowing and shouting in a language[50] the words of which I did not know.
16:1	And I said to the angel, "Where, thus,[51] have you brought me now? For now I can no longer see, because I am weakened and my spirit is departing from me."
16:2	And he said to me, "Remain with me, do not fear!
16:3	He whom you will see going before both of us in a great sound of *qedushah* is the Eternal One who had loved you, whom himself you will not see.
16:4	Let your spirit not weaken <from the shouting>, since I am with you, strengthening you."

ii.ii.ii. Song of Abraham (17)

17:1	And while he was still speaking, behold, a fire was coming toward us round about, and a sound was in the fire like a sound of many waters, like a sound of the sea in its uproar.
17:2	And the angel bowed with me and worshiped.
17:3	And I wanted to fall face down to the earth. And the place of elevation on which we both stood <sometimes was on high,> sometimes rolled down.
17:4	And he said, "Only worship, Abraham, and recite the song which I taught you."
17:5	Since there was no earth to fall to, I only bowed down and recited the song which he had taught me.
17:6	And he said, "Recite without ceasing."

---

[49] CS *народу народъ*—Gk λαόν ὄχλῳ "people in [great] numbers" or Gk ὄχλος λαῶν "crowd of people" (see 1.5.3).

[50] CS *гласъ* 'voice'—Gk φωνή here 'language' Heb לשון (see 1.3.7).

[51] CS *сѣмо* 'here'—Gk ὧδε here 'thus; in this wise'(see 1.3.8).

17:7	And I recited, and he himself recited the song:
17:8	"O, Eternal, Mighty, Holy El, God Autocrat,
17:9	Self-Begotten, Incorruptible, Immaculate, Unbegotten, Spotless, Immortal,
17:10	Self-Created, Self-Illuminated, Without Mother, Without Father, Without Genealogy,
17:11	High, Fiery,
17:12	<Wise>, Lover Of Men, <Favorable,> Generous, Bountiful, Jealous Over Me, Patient, Most Merciful,
17:13	Eli {that is, my God,} Eternal, Mighty, Holy Sabaoth, Most Glorious El, El, El, El, Yahoel.
17:14	You are he whom my soul has loved, the Guardian, Eternal, Fiery, Shining, <Light-Formed>, Thunder-Voiced, Lightning-Looking, Many-Eyed,
17:16	receiving the entreaties of those who honor you <and turning away from the entreaties of those who besiege you by the siege of their provocation,
17:17	releases those who are in the midst of the impious, those who are confused among the unrighteous of the inhabited world in the corruptible life, renewing the life of the righteous>.
17:18	You make the light shine before the morning light upon your creation <from your face in order to bring the day on the earth>.
17:19	And in <your> heavenly dwellings there is an inexhaustible other light of an inexpressible splendor from the lights of your face.[52]
17:20	Accept my prayer, <and let it be sweet to you,> and also the sacrifice which you yourself made to yourself through me who searched for you.
17:21	Receive me favorably and show to me, and teach me, and make known to your servant as you have promised me."

ii.ii.iii. Throne of Glory (18)

18:1	<And> while I was still reciting the song, the edge of the fire which was on the expanse rose up on high.

---

[52] CS свѣтъ сияеши предъ утрьнимъ (SU внутренимъ al.) свѣтомъ на тварь свою (+ и A) отъ лица твоего дневати на земли (отъ... земли om. S) а на небесныхъ жилищихъ твоихъ (om. S) бескуденъ етеръ свѣтъ отъ (om. SAKO) зарьства неисповѣдима отъ свѣтовъ лица твоего—Heb יצירך על הבוקר אור עד אור המאיר מלפניך להביא יום על פני הארץ:ובמשכנות מרומיך שפעת אור אחר מזיו נגהות פניך (see 3.3).

18:2	And I heard a voice like the roaring of the sea, and it did not cease because of the fire.
18:3	And as the fire rose up, soaring higher, I saw under the fire a throne [made] of fire and the many-eyed Wheels,[53] and they are reciting the song. And under the throne [I saw] four singing fiery Living Creatures.
18:4	And their appearance was the same, each one of them had four faces.
18:5	<And> this was the aspect of their faces: of a lion, of a man, of an ox, of an eagle. Four heads <were on their bodies, so that the four Living Creatures had sixteen faces>,
18:6	and each one had six wings: from their shoulders, <and from their sides,> and from their loins.
18:7	With the wings which were from their shoulders they covered their faces, and with the wings from their loins they clothed their feet, and with their middle wings they stretch out straight flying.
18:8	And as they were finishing singing, they looked at one another and threatened one another.
18:9	And it came to pass when the angel who was with me saw that they were threatening each other, he left me and went running to them.
18:10	And he turned the face of each Living Creature from the face which was opposite to it so that they could not see each other's threatening faces.
18:11	And he taught them the song of peace [saying] that everything belonged to the Eternal One.
18:12	While I was still standing and watching, I saw behind the Living Creatures a chariot with fiery Wheels. Each Wheel was full of eyes round about.
18:13	And above the Wheels there was the throne which I had seen. And it was covered with fire and the fire encircled it round about, and an indescribable light surrounded the fiery people.
18:14	And I heard the sound of their qedusha like the voice of a single man.

ii.ii.iv. Celestial Powers (19)

19:1	And a voice came to me out of the midst of the fire, saying, "Abraham, Abraham!"
19:2	And I said, "Here am I!"
19:3	And he said, "Look at the levels which are under the expanse on which you are brought and see that on no single level is there any other but the one whom you have searched for or who has loved you."

---

[53] CS окрьстъ—Gk ΚΥΚΛΟΙ 'wheels' taken for Gk ΚΥΚΛΩΙ 'round about' (see 1.1.3).

19:4	And while he was still speaking, and behold, the levels opened, <and> there are the heavens under me. And I saw on the seventh firmament upon which I stood a fire spread out and light, and dew, and a multitude of angels, and a power of the invisible glory from the Living Creatures which I had seen above. <But> I saw no one else there.
19:5	And I looked from the altitude of my standing to the sixth expanse.
19:6	And I saw there a multitude of incorporeal spiritual angels, carrying out the orders of the fiery angels who were on the eighth firmament, as I was standing on its suspensions.
19:7	And behold, neither on this expanse was there any other power of other form, but only the spiritual angels, and they are the power which I had seen on the seventh firmament.
19:8	And he commanded the sixth expanse to remove itself.
19:9	And I saw there, on the fifth [level], hosts of stars, and the orders they were commanded to carry out, and the elements of earth obeying them."

ii.ii.v. Promise of Seed (20:1–6)

20:1	And the Eternal Mighty One said to me, "Abraham, Abraham!"
20:2	And I said, "Here am I!"
20:3	<And he said,> "Look from on high at the stars which are beneath you and count them for me and tell <me> their number!"
20:4	And I said, "Would[54] I be able? For I am [but] a man."
20:5	And he said to me, "As the number of the stars and their host, so shall I make your seed into a company of nations,[55] set apart for me in my lot with Azazel."

ii.ii.vi. Evil in the World (20:6–23:13)

ii.ii.vi.i. Question (20:6–7)

20:6	And I said, "Eternal Mighty One! Let your servant speak before you and let your fury not rage against your chosen one.
20:7	Behold, before you led me up, Azazel abused me. Why then, while he is now not before you, have you set yourself with him?"[56]

---

[54] CS когда—Gk (εἰ) πότε—אם(ה) (see 1.3.9).
[55] CS положю сѣмени твоему языкъ людии—Heb ושמתי לזרעך את קהל עמים (see 2.3.3.7).

ii.ii.vi.ii. Answer (21:1–23:13)

ii.ii.vi.ii.i. Creation; Chosen People and Peoples of Azazel; Righteous and Sinners (21–22)

21:1	And he said to me, "Look now beneath your feet at the expanse and contemplate the creation which was previously covered over. On this level there is the creation and those who inhabit it and the age that has been prepared to follow it."
21:2	And I looked beneath the expanse at my feet and I saw the likeness of heaven and what was therein.
21:3	And [I saw] there the earth and its fruits, and its moving ones, and its spiritual ones, and its host of men and their spiritual impieties, and their justifications, <and the pursuits of their works,> and the abyss and its torment, and its lower depths, and the perdition which is in it.
21:4	And I saw there the sea and its island<s>, and its animals and its fishes, and Leviathan and his domain, and his lair, and his dens, and the world which lies upon him, and his motions and the destruction of the world because of him.
21:5	I saw there the rivers and their overflows,[57] and their circles.
21:6	And I saw there the tree of Eden and its fruit<s>, and the spring, the river flowing from it, and its trees and their flowering, and I saw those who act righteously. And I saw in it their food and rest.
21:7	And I saw there a great crowd of men, and women, and children, and half of them <on the right side of the portrayal, and half of them> on the left side of the portrayal.
22:1	And I said, "Eternal Mighty One! What is this picture of creation?"
22:2	And he said to me, "This is my will for existence in design, and it was pleasing to me.[58] And then, afterward, I gave them a command by my word and they came into being. And whatever I had determined to be had already been previously depicted and stood before me in this, as you have seen, before they were created.
22:3	And I said, "O Lord! Mighty and Eternal! Who are the people in the picture on this side and on that?"
22:4	And he said to me,

---

[56] CS *како* 'how'—Gk πῶς here 'why' (see 1.3.16).

[57] CS *вышение* lit. 'highness'—Gk ὕψωσις 'highness, majesty'—Heb גאון here 'overflow' (see 2.3.1.2).

[58] CS *и годѣ бысть лицю моему*—Heb וייטב לפני (see 2.3.3.8).

	"These who are on the left side are a multitude of tribes who were before and who are destined to be after you: some for judgment and justice, and others for revenge and perdition at the end of the age.
22:5	Those on the right side of the picture are the people set apart for me of the people [that are] with Azazel. These are the ones I have destined to be born of you and to be called my people."

ii.ii.vi.ii.ii. Fall of Man (23:1–13)

23:1	"Look again at the picture, who is the one who seduced Eve, and what is the fruit of the tree.
23:2	And you will know what will happen, and how, to your seed among people in the last days of the age.
23:3	And what you cannot understand, I shall make known to you what was pleasing to me[59] and I shall tell you the things kept in my heart."
23:4	And I looked at the picture, and my eyes ran to the side of the garden of Eden.
23:5	And I saw there a man very great in height and terrible in breadth, incomparable in aspect, entwined with a woman who was also equal to the man in aspect and size.
23:6	And they were standing under a tree of Eden, and the fruit of the tree was like the appearance of a bunch of grapes of vine.
23:7	And behind the tree was standing, as it were, a serpent in form, but having hands and feet like a man, and wings on its shoulders: six on the right side and six on the left.
23:8	And he was holding in his hands the grapes of the tree and feeding the two whom I saw entwined with each other.
23:9	And I said, "Who are these two entwined with each other, or who is this between them, or what is the fruit which they are eating, Mighty Eternal One?"
23:10	And he said, "This is the reason[60] of men, this is Adam, and this is their desire[61] on earth, this is Eve.
23:11	And he who is between them is the Impiety of their pursuits for destruction, Azazel himself."

---

[59] See 2.3.3.8.
[60] CS с(ъ)вѣтъ—Gk βουλή—Heb עצה, דעת, מחשבה (see 4.3.1).
[61] CS помышьление—Gk ἐπιθυμία—Heb מחמד, or Gk διάνοια—Heb יצר (see 4.3.1).

23:12   And I said, "Eternal Mighty One! Why then did you adjudge to this one such power to destroy humankind by his works on earth?"

23:13   And he said to me, "Hear, Abraham! Those who desire evil and whom I have hated as they are doing[62] these [works], over them I gave him power, and [he is] to be loved by them."

ii.ii.vii. Evil in Man (21:13–26)

ii.ii.vii.i. Question (23:1)

23:14   And I answered and said,

> "Eternal Mighty One!
> Why did you will to do so that evil is desired in the heart of man?
> Since you are angry[63] at what was willed by you,
> who does a bad thing according to your design."

ii.ii.vii.ii. Answer (24–26)

ii.ii.vii.ii.i. Sins of Heathens (24)

24:1   And he said to me,

> "Such is the near future of the nations of peoples which are set apart for you after you from your progeny, as you will see in the picture, what is destined to be with them.

24:2   And I shall tell you what and how it will be in the last days.

24:3   Look now at everything in the picture."

24:4   And I looked and saw there what had been in the world before.

24:5   And I saw, as it were, Adam, and Eve with him, and with them the Evil Adversary and Cain, who acted lawlessly because of the Adversary, and the murdered Abel, the perdition brought and given to him through the Lawless One.

---

[62] CS въторяти—Gk ἐμποιέω (see 1.2.4).

[63] CS гнѣватися + dat.—Gk χολόω/ὀργίζω + dat. (see 1.4.3).

24:6 And I saw there fornication and those who desired it, and its defilement and their jealousy; and the fire of their corruption in the lower depths of the earth.

24:7 And I saw there theft and those who hasten after it, and their judgment <of retribution {that is—of the great court}>.

24:8 I saw there two bare-headed men against me and their shame and the harm against their fellows and their retribution.

24:9 I saw there desire, [and] in its hand the head of every kind of lawlessness <and its torment and its dispersal committed to perdition>.

ii.ii.vii.ii.ii. Sins of Israel (25)

25:1 I saw there the likeness of the idol of jealousy, as a likeness of a craftsman's[64] [work] such as my father made, and its statue was of shining copper, and a man before it, and he was worshiping it;

25:2 and [there was] an altar opposite it and youths were slaughtered on it before[65] the idol.

25:3 And I said to him, "What is this idol, and what is the altar, and who are those being sacrificed, and who is the sacrificer, and what is the beautiful temple which I see, art and beauty of your glory that lies beneath your throne?"

25:4 And he said,

"Hear, Abraham!
This temple and altar and the beautiful things which you have seen are my image of the sanctification of the name of my glory,
where every prayer of men will dwell, and the gathering of kings and prophets,
and the sacrifice which I shall establish to be made for me among my people
coming from your progeny.

25:5 And the statue you saw is my anger, because the people who will come to me out of you will make me angry.

25:6 And the man you saw slaughtering is he who angers me. And the sacrifice is the murder of those who are for me a testimony of the close of the judgment in the end of the creation."

---

[64] CS древодѣля 'carpenter'—Gk τέκτων 'carpenter,' 'craftsman'—Heb חרש here 'smith,' also 'carpenter' (see 1.3.10).

[65] CS въ лице—Gk εἰς (τὸ) πρόσωπον—Heb בפני (see 2.3.2.4).

ii.ii.vii.ii.iii. Free Will and Predetermination (26)

26:1 And I said, "Eternal, Mighty One! Why did you ordain[66] it to be so? Take back these testimonies!"

26:2 And he said to me, "Hear, Abraham, and understand what I tell you, and answer whatever I ask you.

26:3 Why did your father Terah not listen to your voice and abandon the demonic idolatry until he perished, and all his house with him?"

26:4 And I said, "Eternal <Mighty One>! Evidently because[67] he did not will to listen to me, nor did I follow his deeds."

26:5 And he said <to me>,

"Hear, Abraham!
As the will of your father is in him, as your will is in you,
so also the will desired by me[68] is inevitable[69] in coming days
which you will not know in advance, nor the things which are in them.

26:6 You will see with your own eyes what will be with your seed.

26:7 Look at the picture!"

ii.ii.viii. Destiny of Israel (27–32)

ii.ii.viii.i. Destruction of the Temple (27)

27:1 And I looked and saw, and behold, the picture swayed, and a heathen people went out from its left side and they captured those who were on the right side: the men, women, and children.

27:2 <And some they slaughtered> and others they held with them.

27:3 And behold, I saw four hosts[70] coming[71] to them. And they burned the temple with fire, and they carried away[72] the holy things that were in it.[73]

---

[66] CS *основати* 'establish'—Gk θεμελιόω 'establish'—Heb יסד here 'ordain,' 'appoint,' also 'establish' (see 2.3.1.3).

[67] CS *всяко яко*—Gk πάντως ὅτι 'evidently because' (see 1.4.4).

[68] CS *моея воля свѣтъ*—Gk βουλὴ τοῦ θελήματος μοῦ (see 4.4.3).

[69] CS *готовъ бываетъ*—ἕτοιμόν ἐστιν (see 4.4.3).

[70] CS *съхода* or *съходъ*—Gk συναγωγή—Heb מחנה or קהל, or Gk πρέσβυς—Heb מלאך (see 1.2.5).

[71] CS *притещи* 'come'—Gk κατατρέχω here 'descend'(see 1.3.11).

[72] CS *разъграбити* 'plunder'—Gk (δι)αρπάζω here 'seize,' 'take' (see 1.3.12).

27:4 And I said, "Eternal One! The people you have received from me are brought away by the multitudes of peoples.
27:5 And some they are killing and others they are holding as sojourners. And they burned the temple with fire, and they are capturing <and destroying> the beautiful things which are in it.
27:6 Eternal One! If this is so, why have you afflicted my heart and why will it be so?"
27:7 And he said to me, "Listen, Abraham, all that you have seen will happen because of your seed who will provoke me, because of the idol and the murder which you saw in the picture in the temple of jealousy.
27:8 And it will be as you have seen.
27:9 And I said, "Eternal Mighty One! Let the evil works of impiety now pass by, but make commandments in them! Since you can do more than the just works of this [?] !"
27:10 And he said to me,

"Rather the time of justice will come first with the righteousness of kings.
27:11 And I shall adjudge to them with justice those whom I earlier created in order to rule thence[74] over them.[75]
27:12 And from those [kings] will come men who will trouble[76] them, as I made known to you and you saw."[77]

---

[73] CS *се видѣхъ притекшая к нимъ съходы* (SU *въходы al.*) *четыри и цркѵь зажегоша огньмь и сущая в неи стая разграбиша*—Gk καὶ εἶδον τέσσαρα συναγωγὰς [or: τέσσαρας πρέσβεις] κατατρέχοντας πρὸς αὐτοὺς καὶ ἐνέπρεσαν τὸν ναὸν ἐν πυρὶ καὶ ἥρπασαν τὰ ἐν αὐτῷ ὄντα ἅγια—Heb וארא את ארבעה המחנות [אז: המלאכים] יורדים עליהם ויבעירו את המקדש ואת הקדשים אשר בו חטפו (see 1.3.12).

[74] CS *отъ нихъ*—Gk ἐκ τούτων (see 2.3.1.4.)

[75] CS *обладати... в нихъ*—Gk ἐξουσιάζω + ἐν—Heb משל/שלט + ב- (see 2.3.2.3).

[76] CS *потъщати* 'care for'—Gk σπουδάζω 'care for'—Heb הבהיל 'trouble' (see 2.3.1.4.)

[77] CS *и рече къ мнѣ паче праведное время сряшетъ* (SU + *я al.*) *преже преподобьимъ* (SU *подобьимъ al.*) *цѣсарь и въ правдѣ сужу имъ* (SU *судящиимъ al.*) *яже преже създахъ обладати отъ нихъ въ нихъ от техъ же изидутъ мужи иже потъщать* (*потщати* SU) *я елико* (*внелѣже* SU) *възвѣстихъ тебе и видѣ*—Heb ויאמר אלי עוד עת הצדק יבוא בצדקה עם מלכי הצדק: ונתתי להם בצדקה את [העם] אשר יצרתי מראשונה למשול מאז בהם: ומהם יצאו [גם] האישים אשר יבהלום כאשר הודעתיך וראית (see 2.3.1.4.)

ii.ii.viii.ii. Exile (28–29:3)

28:1   And I answered and said, "Mighty <Eternal> One, you who are sanctified in your power, be charitable to my request! As for this reason you made known to me <and showed me [divine secrets] when you have brought me up onto your height,

28:2   so for the same reason make it known to me>, your beloved, what I ask: whether what I saw will happen to them for long?"

28:3   And he showed me a multitude of his people

28:4   and said to me, "For this reason, my anger at them will come through the four hosts which you saw, and through them will come retribution from me for their works.

28:5   And in the fourth host there are one hundred years and also one hour of the age. And for one hundred years it will be in evil [circumstances] among the heathen <and an hour in their mercy and agreement[78] as among the heathen>.

29:1   And I said, "Eternal <Mighty> One! How long a time is an hour of the age?"

29:2   And he said, "I set twelve periods for this impious age to rule over[79] the heathens and over your seed, and what you have seen will be until the end of time.

29:3   And reckon and you will know. Look into the picture!"

ii.ii.viii.iii. False and True Messiahs (29:4–13)

29:4   <And I looked> and saw a man going out from the left side of the heathen. Men and women and children, great crowds, went out from the side of the heathen and they worshiped him.

29:5   <And> while I was still looking, those on the right side went out, and some shamed this man, and some struck him, and some worshiped him.

29:6   <And> I saw that as they worshiped him, Azazel ran and worshiped, and having kissed his face he turned and stood behind him.

29:7   And I said, "Eternal Mighty One! Who is this shamed and struck man, worshiped by the heathen with Azazel?"

29:8   And he answered and said,

"Hear, Abraham, the man whom you saw shamed and struck and again worshiped is the laxity[80] of the heathen for the people who

---

[78] CS *съпоношение*—Gk σύμβασις 'agreement' (see 1.2.6).
[79] CS *држати въ*—Heb שלט + ‏-ב‎ (see 2.3.2.3).
[80] CS *ослаба* 'relaxing'—Gk ἔκλυσις, παράλυσις here 'laxity' or ἄνεσις 'willfulness' (see 1.3.13).

	will come from you in the last days, in this twelfth hour of the age of impiety.
29:9	And in the [same] twelfth period of the close of my age I shall set up the man from your seed which you saw.
29:10	Everyone from my people will [finally] admit him, while the sayings of him who was as if called by me will be neglected in their minds.
29:11	And that you saw going out from the left side of the picture and those worshiping him, this [means that] many of the heathen will hope in him.
29:12	<And> those of your seed you saw on the right side, some shaming and striking him, and some worshiping him, many of them will be misled on his account.
29:13	And he will tempt those of your seed who have worshiped him.

ii.ii.viii.iv. Judgment and Salvation (29:14–21)

29:14	In the close of the twelfth hour, in the ceasing of the age of impiety, before the age of justice will start to grow, my judgment will come upon the heathen who have acted wickedly through the people of your seed who have been set apart for me.
29:15	In those days I shall bring upon all earthly creation ten plagues through evil and disease and the groaning of the bitterness of their soul,[81]
29:16	as I shall bring upon the generations of men who are on it [= earth], because of the anger and the corruption of their deeds with which they provoke me.
29:17	And then from your seed will the righteous men be left, kept by me by number,[82] hastening in the glory of my name to the place prepared beforehand for them, which you saw deserted in the picture.
29:18	And they will live, being sustained[83] by the sacrifices and the offerings of justice and truth in the age of justice.
29:19	And they will rejoice over me forever, and they will destroy those who have destroyed them, and they will rebuke those who have rebuked them by mockery,

---

[81] CS *горесть душа ихъ*—Heb מרת נפשם (see 2.3.3.2).
[82] CS *въ чисмени* lit. "in number"—Gk ἐν ἀριθμῷ—Heb במספר "by [exact] count" or "in [prescribed] number" (see 2.3.3.9).
[83] CS *утврьдити* 'sustain' (29:18)—Gk στηρίζω 'sustain' also with food—Heb סעד 'sustain with food' (see 1.3.14).

29:20	and those who spit in their faces will be rebuked by me, when they will see me joyfully rejoicing with my people and receiving those who return to me <in repentance>.
29:21	See, Abraham, what you have seen, and <hear> what you have heard, and know <what you have known>. Go to your lot! And behold, I am with you forever."

ii.ii.viii.v. Punishment of Heathens and Gathering of Israel (30–31)

30:1	And while he was still speaking, I found myself on the earth, and I said, "Eternal, Mighty One, I am no longer in the glory in which I was above, but what my soul desired to understand I do not understand in my heart."
30:2	And he said to me,
	"Abraham, I shall tell [you] what your heart desired, for you have sought to know the ten plagues which I prepared against the heathen, and I prepared them beforehand after the passing of the twelve hours on earth.
30:3	Hear what I tell you, it will be thus.
30:4	The first—distress from much violence; the second—the fiery burning of cities;
30:5	the third—destruction of the cattle by pestilence; the fourth—famine in their native land,
30:6	the fifth—destruction in their domains[84] through the ravage of earthquake and sword; the sixth—hail and increase of snow;
30:7	the seventh—wild beasts will be their grave; the eighth—famine and pestilence will take turns in their destruction;
30:8	the ninth—punishment by the sword and flight in distress; the tenth—thunder and voices, and ravaging earthquakes.
31:1	Then I shall sound the trumpet from the sky, and I shall send my chosen one, having in him one measure of all my power, and he will summon my people blamed among the heathen.

---

[84] CS *владыка* 'ruler'—Gk εξουσία here 'domain'—Heb מדינה (see 1.3.15).

31:2	And I shall burn with fire those who mocked them ruling over[85] them in this age and I shall commit those who have covered me with mockery to the reproach of the coming age.
31:3	Since I have destined them to be food for the fire of hell, and ceaseless soaring in the air of the underground depths, <the contents of a worm's belly.
31:4	For those who do justice, who have chosen my will and clearly kept my commandments, will see them.[86] And they will rejoice with joy at the destruction of the abandoned.
31:5	And those who followed after the idols and after their murders will rot in the womb of the Evil One—the belly of Azazel, and they will be burned by the fire of Azazel's tongue.
31:6	Since I waited until they came to me, and they did not want it.
31:7	And they glorified an alien.
31:8	And they joined one to whom they had not been allotted, and they abandoned the prevailing Lord.
31:9	Therefore, hear, Abraham, and see! Behold, your seventh generation will go with you.
31:10	And they will go out into an alien land.
31:11	And they will be enslaved and distressed for about one hour of the impious age.
31:12	And of the people whom they will serve—I am the judge.">

---

[85] CS *властьствующая въ нихъ* (lit. "rule in/among)—Heb מושלים/שולטים בהם (see 2.3.2.3).

[86] CS *узрятъ бо въ нихъ*—Heb יראו בהם (see 2.3.2.3).

Chapter 1
Greek Vorlage

Like nearly all early Slavonic literary texts, *ApAb* was translated from the Greek. Apart from general historical considerations this conclusion may be confirmed by the long lists of Hellenisms. The most obvious Hellenisms common to a wide range of Slavonic texts are adduced by RL (686) and Lunt (1985:56). In this work we are concerned with the retroversion of those Greek counterparts which are not obvious or common, and/or the reconstruction of which contributes to our understanding of the document. Below we present examples for each type of the translation phenomena which make the retroversion possible, namely: (1) graphic misinterpretations, (2) morphological calques (3) semantic calques, (4) syntactic Hellenisms, and (5) phraseological Hellenisms.

1.1. Graphic misinterpretations

1.1.1.   *CS* коконилъ *(2:3)*
         Gk κόκκον Νείλου *(in* scriptio continua—*κοκκουνειλου)*

In 2:3 Abraham goes out to the "main road" in order to sell his father's idols, "and behold, merchants from Paddan Aram came with camels to go to Egypt to buy *kokonil* [?] from the Nile there"—*и се купци отъ фанданы сурьскыя грядутъ съ вельблуды идуще въ египетъ куповатъ оттудѣ коконилъ* (AD: *куконилъ* C *вконилъ* BKO *погонилъ* I) *от нила* (*оттудѣ... нила* om. SU). Rub suggests that *hapax legomenon коконилъ* is the calque from Gk κοκκίνα 'scarlet clothing' or κουκίνος 'doum palm; fiber of palm,' which does not help to explain the origin of all constituent parts of the word. We propose to interpret *коконилъ* as a combination of two words which could be either original Greek or their Slavonic transliterations attested in other documents. The Greek *Vorlage* probably contained: *) ἀγοράζειν κόκκον Νείλου (in *scriptio continua*—*κοκκουνειλου; unattested elsewhere) with the regular Middle Greek itacism reading of the diphthong ει (for other cases of incorrect division of words in Slavonic translations see Thomson 1988a:360). CS *кокъ* reproducing Gk κόκκος occurs in the 15th cent. East Slavic mss of *De Bello Judaico* (Мещерский 1958:70). There it means 'scarlet,' denoting one of the cloths from which the veil in the Temple was made—Heb שני or תולעת שני

(Exod 25:4 *et pass.*). In our case its later meaning—'grain'—is no less appropriate to the context. The word is known as 'wheat grain' (see, e.g., Philumenus, *De Venenatis Animalibus* 3:3—LSJ:971) and as 'barley' in later sources (Sophocles 1860:380). Egypt's grain export is reflected not only in Gen 41ff. but was also a well-known part of the Hellenistic world. The merging of κόκκον and Νείλου into one word and, perhaps, the dittographic writing of Νείλου might have appeared in the *Vorlage* as well as at the stage of translation. Neither can the following reading be rejected: ἀγοράζειν κόκκον Νείλου ἀπὸ Νείλου 'to buy the Nile's grain from the Nile.'

1.1.2. CS усѣчи *'behead' (1:9)*
Gk πελεκάω *'hew' taken for* πελεκίζω *'behead'*

The verse 1:9 is very obscure: *и усѣче другаго марумафу отъ другаго камени безъ главы и главу отъвергъшююся отъ марумафа и прочее марумафы* (*и прочее марумафы* : om. A) *скруши*—lit. "[Trying to improve the damage injured to his idol Mar-Umath] he [Terah] carved another Mar-Umath, out of another stone, without a head, and [placed on him] the head that had been thrown down from Mar-Umath, and smashed the rest of Mar-Umath." Bonw solves almost all of the problems of its interpretation by translating *усѣчи* as "bildete" and proposing to insert *положи на нь* after *отъ марумафа*. According to this reading only the torso of the idol was damaged (see *Translation*). This interpretation conforms to the contents of 3:6,8: "his [Mar-Umath's] head fell off of him. And he [Terah] put it on another stone of another god, which he had made without a head.... How then can my father's god Mar-Umath, having the head of one stone and being made of another stone, save a man, or hear a man's prayer and reward him?" [1] The shortcoming of Bonwetsch's reading, nevertheless, is that *усѣчи*, unlike *сѣчи*, does not occur elsewhere in CS documents with the meaning 'cut, carve.' It was widely used to denote 'cut off'—ἐκκόπτω and more specifically: 'behead'—ἀποκεφαλίζω (according to Srezn and Mikl it was mostly used in the latter meaning). The only way to stay with the interpretation of Bonwetsch is to assume that the Slav translator has taken πελεκάω 'hew,' 'shape with an ax' (Heb פסל, 3 Kgdms 6:1=1 Kgs 5:32) for the more familiar πελεκίζω 'behead,' which is found in the NT; cf. Rev 20:4 (the forms of historical tenses of these verbs look almost identical).

---

[1] If we try to avoid the interpolation of *положи на нь*, still treating *усечи* as 'cut, carve,' we must assume that Terah made some kind of headless idol or that the CS prototext had *без главизны*—ἄνευ κιδάρεως; cf. EpJer 9 about crowns (στεφάνοι) for idols. But these speculations contradict the evidence of 3:6.

1.1.3. CS окрьстъ *(18:3)*
Gk ΚΥΚΛΟΙ *'wheels' taken for Gk* ΚΥΚΛΩΙ *'round about'*

In his heavenly journey Abraham saw *многоочесныхъ окрьстъ*, lit. "many-eyed round about" (18:3), which might go back to Gk πλήρεις ὀφταλμῶν κυκλόθεν—Heb מלאים עינים סביב (Ezek 1:18; 10:12). Cf. 18:12: *коеждо коло полно очесъ окр̅стъ* "each Wheel was full of eyes round about."[2] Here, however, the phrase looks elliptic: *и видѣхъ подъ огнемъ престолъ* (SU: + *и al.*) *отъ огня и* (SU: om. *al.*) *многоочесныхъ окрьстъ*. "Many-eyed Wheels" (Heb אופנים מלאים עינים) of Ezek 10:12 must be meant: the Slav translator took the nom. pl. κύκλοι (ΚΥΚΛΟΙ in unical script) 'wheels' for the adv. κύκλῳ (ΚΥΚΛΩΙ) 'round about.' The confusion of *o* and *ω* is well attested in Slavonic translations; cf., e.g., CS *якоже* (Gk ὡς) in place of Gk ὅς (*Ephr. Syr.* 30; *Supr* 517—Thomson 1988a:358).

1.2. Morphological calques

1.2.1. CS *настрьзати *(1:1)*
Gk ἐπικείρω *'destroy'*

The writing begins with the following words: *въ дьнь настрьзающю* (*настръзающи* В *настерзающи* AD *настерезающи* СК) *ми богы отьца фары* "On the day when I was <?> the gods of my father Terah...." The phrase contains the *hapax legomenon настръзати/настрьзати*. *Lectiones difficiliores* in mss S (*настръзающю*) and В (*настръзающи*) may be considered as closest to the prototext, while AD apparently reflect an East Slavic development of *-ьr-* > *-er-*, and CK contain the forms reflecting the secondary *polnoglasie* or the analogous influence of **stьrzǫ, *stergti*. (cf. Lunt 1985:58). The root of the *hapax* cannot be determined exactly; there are at least three different possibilities. In previous research the root was considered to be *stьrg/sterg/storg* 'guard'; it was argued that the mutation of *g* to **z* is more usual with front-vowel roots (Lunt 1985:58). Actually, the palatalization of the root-final consonant might be conditioned morphologically (see Troubetzkoy 1922; Vondrák 1923/24; Otrębski 1948; Shevelov 1964:339–344). Thus, the root **strug-/*strъg-* 'carve' becomes also possible. Taking into consideration that CS *стръгати* (attested also in the form *стръзати* < **stъrzati*; see Mikl:893), usually rendered Gk ξέω/ξύω (Slov:4.186; Srezn:3.562; LSJ:649), and that Slavonic calques prefixed by *на-*, as a rule, reproduce Greek forms with ἐπι- (see, e.g., Srezn: 2.266–353), **настръзати* might have reproduced Gk ἐπιξέω

---

[2] For a broader context here and elsewhere see *Translation*.

or ἐπιξύω. Cf. ἐπιξύω used with εἰκόνες λίθῳ "stone images" (Procopius Caesariensis, *De Aedificiis*—LSJ:649). Terah is described as an idol-maker in parallel sources (*Jub* 12, *Tanna debe Eliahu* 2:25, *Gen. Rab.* 38:13), and, moreover, Abraham himself is depicted as making an idol with his father in *Seder Eliahu Rabba* (= *Dibrei Yemei Yerahmiel*) 33.

However, the most probable root seems to be *strig-/*strьg(?). Here also phonological conditions for the progressive palatalization are observed; cf. the forms of the same root with palatalization after *i: *постризати* (Vaillant 1966:2.167), *постризание* (Srezn:2.1267). Gk κείρω was known to Slav scribes in its principal meaning, 'cut hair' (Srezn:2.571; Vasmer:3.778). Thus, CS *настрьзати might render Gk ἐπικείρω 'destroy' (LSJ:637,932; Lampe:740). Cf. an analogous model: *постригати* for ἀποκείρω (Srezn:2.1266). This meaning seems to be the most appropriate to the context: Abraham destroys idols in *ApAb* 1:6; 2:9; 5:6–7; 8:5–6, in Palaia interpolations borrowed from the *Chronicle of George the Monk* in *ApAb* 8 (mss ABCK) and in other midrashic and apocryphal sources: *Gen. Rab.* 38:19; *Tanna debe Eliahu* 2:25; *Jub* 12 (cf. *ApAb* 8:5–6). In this case *настрьзати* may be defined as both a morphological and semantic calque.[3]

1.2.2. CS прѣмыслити *(5:1)*
Gk κατανοέω
Heb צפה, ראה *'see'*

"And when he [Terah] heard my [Abraham's] word, his anger was kindled against me, since I had spoken harsh words against his gods. When I <?> [*прѣмысливъ* (*прѣмыслихъ* SU)] my father's anger, I went out" (4:5–5:1). Lunt (1985:57) posits a West Slavic origin for *прѣмыслити*. Its sense attested in Czech and Slovene was considered by Bonw ("überdenken") and by most of the later translators apparently following him: "think over" (BL), "ponder" (RL), "songer" (Phil). We have not found any justification for this meaning in East or South Slavic languages. Srezn (2.1670) translates *прѣмыслити* of *ApAb* as "обмануть," apparently implying the meaning of Gk κατασοφίζομαι, which renders Heb התחכם in Exod 1:10. Srezn presents also the meaning "предусмотреть" (καταπραγματεύω in *Greg. Niss.* 11th cent.). Rub and Pennington translate *прѣмыслихъ* correspondingly "ayant pris en considération" and "took notice." This interpretation reflects one of the meanings of Gk ἐπινοέω usually rendered by CS *примыслити* (Slov:3:289; Srezn:2.1432–1434).

The only possible Semitic equivalent seems to be one of the verbs with the meaning 'see.' They are rendered by Gk κατανοέω (Gk κατα- > CS *прѣ/при*,

---

[3] For the detailed disscussion on the *hapax* see Kulik 1997a.

Gk νοέω > CS мыслити): ראה (Gen 42:9; Exod 2:11, etc.), צפה (Ps 37(36):32), Aram חזה הוה (Dan 7:21).

1.2.3. CS съпримѣрение (< *съпримѣренье) (6:9)
Gk συμμετρότερος 'more proportional'

In his reflection on the hierarchy of idols Abraham says:
что же иоавонѣ бозѣ на друзѣмъ бозѣ (на друзѣмъ бозѣ om. SU) иже стоитъ съ зухеемъ яко и чьстнъ есть паче варисаиа бога иже есть отъ дрѣва дѣланъ и отъ сребра кованъ яко тъ съпримирение есть (В спрімѣренье A спримѣреніе K om. SU) цѣниванъ(om. SU) отъ чловѣкъ на явление видения

"[And] what about Yoavon, a god <who is in the power of another god>,[4] who stands beside Zoukh? <Since [even] he is more honored than the god Bar-Eshath who is made of wood, while [Yoavon is] forged of silver. And *being better proportioned* [?], he is sold by men in order to show him>" (6:9)[5]

CS съпримирение is a *hapax legomenon*. Mikl has примѣрение "admetiri" (673), Srezn: примѣрятися (2.1434). They both are derived from *měr-* and should render Gk συν- + -μετρ-: συμμετρία, συμμετρέω, etc. (cf. RL). Our text would be clearer if we were to presume that the prototext contained the comparative form **съпримѣренье* (a calque of Gk συμμετρότερος) which, due to the well attested interchange of и/ѣ, was understood by later copyists as the noun *съпримирение*.[6]

1.2.4. CS вътворяти (23:13)
Gk ἐμποιέω 'do,' 'produce'

In 23:12–13 Abraham says: "'Eternal Mighty One! Why then did you adjudge to this one [Azazel] such power to destroy humankind by his works on earth?' And he said to me, 'Hear, Abraham! Those who desire evil and whom I have hated as they are doing these [works] [елико възненавидехъ въ творящихъ я], over them I gave him power, and [he is] to be loved by them.'"

---

[4] Here and elsewhere the portions of text which do not occur in the version of *Codex Sylvester* (ms S) are enclosed in triangular brackets.
[5] For interpretation of the entire verse see 4.5.1.
[6] Alternative interpretations: (1) Gk σύμμετρος in Aq Jer 22:14 renders Heb מדות meaning 'big' in בית מדות "big house." Thus, ᴙ might have בעל מדות 'big'; cf. אנשי מדות (Num 13:32); (2) The meanings 'of wreathed work' or 'strung together' (Gk συνειρόμενος) are less probable (cf. πλοκή in Exod 28:14 and further): assuming a root *mir-*, we could posit that συνείρω was taken for συν- + -ειρην- (CS мировати, смирение).

In the second verse there is an unusual prepositional government of *възненавидети* + *въ*. With another word division CS *вътворяти/вътваряти* (Mikl:112; Srezn:1.433) may be a calque of Gk ἐμποιέω.

1.2.5. CS съхода *(27:3)*
Gk συναγωγή

In the historical part of his vision Abraham observes the destruction of the Temple: *и се видѣхъ притекшая к нимъ съходы* (SU *въходы al.*) *четыри и цр͞квь зажегоша огньмь и сущая в неи стая разграбиша*—"And behold, I saw four hosts [?] coming to them [to the people on the right side of the visionary picture]. And they burned the temple with fire, and they carried away [on this word see below 1.3.6–7] the holy things that were in it" (27:3). The most problematic word in this verse in an enigmatic *съходы* translated here as "hosts" (cf. *въсходъ* (*входъ* A) in 25:4, *сходы* (*исходы* A) in 28:4 and *сходъ* (*входъ* ACKO) in 28:5). The combination *съходы четыри* may be interpreted as masc. as well as fem. acc. pl. There is an almost identical verse in Slavonic *LadJac*, where the majority reading contains the form *сходы* (and not *въходы*): *пусто сътворитъ место се сходи д-ми* "this place will be desolated by the four <?>" (*LadJac* 5:7). *LadJac* 5:9 has *въсходы* like in *ApAb* 25:4: *храмъ имени бога твоего ... запустѣетъ въсходы д*: "a Temple in the name of your God ... will be devastated by four <?>." Mikl and Srezn define *съходы* of *ApAb* as fem. (Mikl apparently identifies it with *схода* 'scout' from the 16th century *Vita Alexandri*). Bonw proposes "durch vier Eingange" based on his reading *въходы* of later mss as instr., which contradicts the form of the numeral (*четыри*). BL follow Bonw in translation ("through four entrances"), but note that *съходы* may mean 'descents,' 'generations' (hypothetical Heb תצאות). Lunt (RL:702) proposes to emend *съходы* to *исходы* "exits" or *въсходы* "ascents," and *четыри* also to instr.—*четырьми*.

Rub reconstructs for *схода* Gk κατάσκοπος (as in *Vita Alexandri*, Mikl:964)—Heb מלאך 'angel,' relying upon the only precedent in Josh 6:24(25), where κατάσκοπος 'scout' of LXX corresponds to מלאך 'messenger,' 'angel' of MT. Rub relies on the midrashic story of four angels burning the First Temple (*Pesiqta Rabbati* 26,131; *2 Bar* 6:4–5; for other sources see Ginzberg 1909–1938:6.392–394). Four angels represent four kingdoms in *Lev. Rab.* 29:2 and parallels; and the four kingdoms carry out or mark God's punishment of Israel in Abraham's vision according to Targum Neophyti *ad* Gen 15:12 (cf. *Mekhilta de R. Ishmael, Yitro* (Bahodesh 9)). In support of Rub we can bring CS *сходьникъ*, which reproduces Gk κατάσκοπος in Slavonic NT (*Christ, Slepč, Šiš* Heb 11:31; and as a gloss to *прѣлогатай* in *Vita Alexandri, ibid.*) as well as ἄγγελος itself, both in East and South Slavic versions of the Epistle of James, relating to the same story of Josh 6 (*Christ, Šiš* Jac 2:25; see Slov:3.362; Mikl:965).

It should be taken into consideration, however, that the translation of LXX in Josh 6:24(25) is contextual, and "messenger" there is, at the same time, "scout" according to the plot. We suppose that CS *съходъ* or *съхода* must be rather a calque of Gk συν- or κατα- + a verb with the meaning 'go.' Gk (συγ)κατάβασις 'descent,' or esp. σύνοδος or συναγωγή 'gathering' may be also appropriate to the context (here as well as in 25:4; see comm. *ibid.*). Gk συναγωγή regularly translated by CS *съньмъ* may mean 'gathering/host [of angels]'; see Srezn:2.780: *ангелъ съньмъ* (*Irmolog.* 1250), *сьнемъ свяштенъ* (*Supr* 72). Cf. Heb קְהַל קְדֹשִׁים (Ps 89:6) or רִבְבוֹת קֹדֶשׁ (Deut 33:2). Therefore, here "hosts [of angels]" might also be meant. In LXX Gk συναγωγή regularly renders Heb (ה)קהל, עדה, המון (only in Dan), and less frequently אספה/אסף (Exod 32:22,21), מחנה (Num 5:2—according to Cod. Alex. while Cod. Vat. has Gk παρεμβολή, a regular equivalent of Heb מחנה), סוד (Jer 6:11), חיל (Ezek 37:9). ארבע מחנות שכינה "[angelic] camps of Shekhina" and particularly ארבע מחנות שכינה "four camps of Shekhina" are found in *3 En* 18:4; 37:1. Cf. "four Presences" (*1 En* 40:8–10), "four ranks" in heaven (*2 En* 18:9(*a*), "four rows" of angels (*3 En* 18:4), "four companies of ministering angels" (*Masekhet Hekhalot* 6, Jellinek 1853–1878:2.43).

CS *съхода/съходъ* may also be a calque of one of the following Greek words: πρέσβυς, πρεσβεύς, πρεσβευτής, πρεσβεία meaning 'messenger,' 'embassy': Gk πρεσβεία was rendered by CS *съхождение* in *Greg. Naz.* 11th cent. 86 (Srezn:3.862). In LXX Gk πρέσβυς reproduces Heb מלאך 'messenger,' 'angel' (Num 21:20(21); 22:25; Deut 2:26).

1.2.6. CS съпоношение *(28:5)*
Gk σύμβασις *'agreement'*

In 28:5 the protagonist is informed about the terms and conditions of the future exile of Israel: *р҃ лѣтъ будеть въ злѣ въ языцѣхъ а часъ въ милость ихъ и споношении (поношении* B; *а часъ ... споношении* om. S)—"for one hundred years[7] it [Israel] will be in evil among the heathen <and an hour in their mercy and agreement>. The verse is obscure. *Hapax legomenon споношение* previously understood, according to evidence of ms B, as *поношение* (Gk ὄνειδος, Heb חרפה/כלימה) 'reproach' is rather a calque of Gk σύμβασις

---

[7] "Year" here and "hour" below designate relative periods of time used in eschatological descriptions in *ApAb*. Chronological units which occur in the eschatological portion of *ApAb* (28:5; 29:1,2,13,14,18; 30:2; 31:2; 32:3) are as follows: CS *лѣто*—Gk ἐνιαυτός—Heb שנה 'year/cycle'; CS *часъ*—Gk ὥρα – Heb שעה 'hour'; CS *годъ/година*—Gk καιρός—Heb זמן/עת 'period of time' (used as a synonym for *часъ* 'hour' in 29:2,9); CS *вѣкъ*—Gk αἰών—Heb דור/עולם 'age.'

'agreement,' 'coming together' (LSJ:1675; Lampe:1280; cf. CS съпонести for Gk συμβαστάζω in Job 28:19—Srezn:3:800).

1.3. Semantic calques[8]

1.3.1.   *CS* свѣтъ *'light' (5:8)*
        Gk φῶς *here 'fire'*

See 1.5.2.

1.3.2.   *CS* дѣло *'work' (7:7)*
        derivation from Gk ἐργάζωμαι *here 'plow' (Heb* עבד*)*

The earth is "made for men to plow"—челкомъ на дѣло учинена ес̃, lit. "made for men to work." CS дѣло renders here Gk ἐργασία or other derivation from ἐργάζωμαι, which, as well as Heb עבד, means both 'work' and 'plow.'

1.3.3.   *CS* убагрити *'make s.-th. red' (7:12)*
        Gk πορφύρω *here 'color'*

Abraham defines God as one "who made the heaven purple" (*иже убогъри* (SU *убагри al.*) *нбс̃а*. Here, however, CS *убагрити* rendering Gk πορφύρω must imply another kind of mollusk-produced dye: "who colored the heaven"; cf. Gk ὁλοπόρφυρος rendering Heb תכלת 'blue' in LXX Num 4:7. Thus, "who made the heaven blue" is also possible.

1.3.4.   *CS* преже вѣка *'before the world' (9:3)*
        Gk ἕως εἰς τὸν αἰῶνα
        Heb עד עולם *here 'for ever'*

In the beginning of the revelation God characterizes himself this way: *азъ есмь преже вѣка и крѣпокъ бг̃ъ иже первѣе створихъ свѣта вѣка* (S *иже преже створихъ първѣе свѣта вѣка* ABC *иже преже первѣе створихъ свѣта вѣка* D)—"I am the primordial and mighty God, who initially [?] created

---

[8] For examples of the "wrong choice of meaning of a polysemantic word" in other Slavonic translations from Greek see Thomson (1988a:368–370); cf. Molnár (1985), Schumann (1950).

the two luminaries [?] of the world [?]" (9:3). For CS *преже вѣка* Rub proposes the quite rare Gk προαιώνιος (rendered usually by *прѣвѣчьныи* (Slov:3.414; Srezn:2.1626), that occurs also in our document in 13:8,10), and Heb אלהי קדם or קדמון. CS pl. *преже вѣкъ* 'before the ages/worlds' is well attested for rendering Gk πρὸ τῶν αἰώνων (1 Cor 2:7, SDRJa11–14:2.293). Sg. *преже вѣка* here might have rendered Gk ἕως εἰς τὸν αἰῶνα (Heb עד עולם), usually reproduced by CS *до вѣка* (Srezn:1.485). This wide-spread Hebrew/Greek biblical idiom meaning "for eternity" relates to the future rather than to a preceding eternal existence. Thus, the verse as a whole may be a transposition paraphrase of Ps 136:7:

| ... to him who created the great luminaries, for his mercy is forever (Ps 135:7) | I am forever... who initially created the two luminaries of the world (*ApAb* 9:3) |

1.3.5. CS *свѣта* dual. *'lights'* (9:3)
Gk φῶτα *here 'luminaries' (Heb* (מ)ורות*))*

In the same verse (cf. 1.3.4.) we translated CS *свѣта* as "two luminaries." If CS *свѣта* is interpreted as gen. sg. 'light,' Gk φωτός and *первѣе (пръвѣе)* as 'before,' Gk πρό (Slov:3.401; Mikl:715), the verse might be translated like this: "who (previously) created before the light of the world" (see RL). CS *свѣта вѣка*, thus, would go back to Heb אור עולם, lit. 'light of the world/eternity' = 'eternal light.' Cf. Isa 60:19,20: "the Lord will be your eternal light [φῶς αἰώιον, אור עולם]," and John 8:12: "I am the light of the world [τὸ φῶς τοῦ κόσμου]." In our case, however, this definition seems to be less plausible, for in both cited sources it is an epithet of God himself. This problem may be solved by the following assumption. The form of CS *вѣка* is identical with that of the previous word *свѣта*, and the semantic fields of both intersect (in the meaning 'world'). Thus, *вѣка* might be a gloss for *свѣта*, inserted by a Slav scribe in order to indicate that *свѣтъ* here means not 'light' (Gk φῶς, Heb אור) but 'world' (Gk κόσμος/αἰών, Heb עולם; see Slov:4.35; Srezn:3.297). For this scribe the passage would mean: "who created before the world/eternity," while the prototext would read: *иже первѣе створихъ свѣта* which may be understood also as "who created before the light [was existing]" (or even "before man" considering that the gen. of Gk φῶς 'light' and φώς 'man' are identical—φωτός).

In any case, the difficulty of the above readings is the absence of an object for the transitive verb *створихъ* "create." The scribe of ms K tried to solve the problem by interpolating here "heaven and earth," which were created before the light and world. The only reasonable candidate for the role of a verbal object in the text at hand may be *свѣта*, understood as acc. dual. 'two lights/luminaries.' The word for 'light' denotes sometimes also 'luminary' in Slavonic (*свѣтъ*, Slov:4.35; Srezn:3.296), as well as in Greek (φῶς, and not only in Jewish

Hellenistic sources; see, e.g., τὰ φῶτα meaning sun and moon in Ptolemaeus, *Tetrabiblos* 37,38) and Heb (אורים in Ps 136:7). Thus, God is defined here by the creation of luminaries, for they were Abraham's last candidates for gods, considered by him to be the most powerful elements of the world (see 7:8–10; cf. 7:12). Taking further into account that CS *первѣе* (*пръвѣе*) was widely used as an adv. 'initially, primarily' rendering Gk πρῶτον/πρῶτος (see Slov, Srezn and Mikl:*ibid.*), Heb (ב)ראשונה, בתחילה (Judg 20:32; Dan 8:1; Aq Th Isa 65:7; Jer 16:18, etc.) or Gk πρότερον (Slov:3.401; Srezn:2.1768; Mikl:715), Heb לפנים (Lev 18:27; Deut 2:12; Josh 1:14; Jer 34(41):5; Neh 13:5), בראשונה (1 Kgs 13:6; Jer 33(40):11), מראשית (Isa 46:10), קדם (Jer 30(33):20), we get the linguistically plausible and intertextually confirmed interpretation based on the oldest ms: "who initially created the two luminaries of the world" (*иже первѣе створихъ свѣта вѣка* S). For "who created the luminaries" (*створихъ свѣта*) see Ps 136(135):7: "to him who created great luminaries"—τῷ ποιήσαντι φῶτα μεγάλα—לעשה אורים גדלים (cf. previous commentary); for "the luminaries of the world" (*свѣта вѣка*) see *3 En* 10 (Schäfer 1981:#13,V48a/12): מאורות שבעולם "the luminaries that are in the world"; *Gen. Rab.* 12,5: מאורות ארץ "the luminaries of the earth." Thus, this passage in Hebrew might look like this: אשר מראשית ברא (מ)אורות עולם.

1.3.6. CS поновения *(9:9)*
Gk ἐγκαίνια 'consecration,' 'holiday of consecration'
Heb חנוכה

Having been ordered to fulfill the sacrifice ("Covenant Between the Pieces"), Abraham gets the promise of the historical vision: *и ту покажу ти вѣкы гломъ моимъ създаная и утверженая сътвореная и поновеная*—"and there I shall show you the ages: the things built and firmed, made and renewed by my word" (9:9). Ms S has *създания и утвержения сътворения и поновения*, lit. "constructings and strengthenings, makings and renovations" (thus, the beginning of the verse must be: "and there I shall show you the ages by my word"). The fourth term CS *поновения* 'renovations' may reproduce Gk ἐγκαίνια (like *поновления* in *Supr* 239,6; Mikl:623) and Heb חנוכה 'consecration'; cf. LXX and MT in Dan 3:2; Ezra 6:16,17; Neh 12:27 (in the last two cases the consecration of the Second Temple is meant). In John 10:22 this Greek word (as well as its Hebrew counterpart in rabbinic sources) was used to denote the feast of Chanukah established by Judas Maccabaeus at the reconsecration of the Temple after the Maccabean revolt. Thus, the other three terms may also relate to the stages of the history of Israel classified according to the destiny of the Temple: (1) "constructions"—CS *съзьдание* 'creation' (Gk κτῆσις), 'creature' (Gk πλάσμα) was used to translate Greek words meaning 'building' or 'process of building': Gk οἰκοδομή—Heb מבנה (Ezek 40:2), בירה (1 Chr 29:1), בנין (Aq Sm Ezek 40:5), בית (Th Ezek 11:1) designating the

Temple, or Gk οἰκοδόμησις, οἰκοδομία (cf. *създание храмины* "the building of the house" in *Pand. Ant.* 11th cent., 251). Thus, here the foundation of the Temple of Solomon may be meant; cf. the description of the celestial prototype of the Temple in 25:4. (2) "Strengthenings"—*утвержения* (Gk ἀσφάλεια?)— restoration of the offerings or repair of the Temple (cf., e.g., 2 Kgs 12:5–16) by the righteous kings of the First Temple period; cf. 27:10: "the time of justice will come with the righteousness of kings ...." (3) "Makings"—*сътворения* Gk ποίησις (Heb מעשה) or ἀποτέλεσμα 'completion,' 'accomplishment' (Slov:4.351; Mikl:958)—building of the Second Temple. Cf. the four stages of the Jewish history in *ApAb* with the analogous triple structures in *1 En* and *2 Bar*:

ApAb 9:9:	*1 En*:	*2 Bar*:
1) "constructings"	1) 89:59 First Temple	1) 61 First Temple
2) "strengthenings"	2) --	2) 66 restorations of the offering
3) "makings"	3) 89:72 Second Temple	3) 68 Second Temple
4) "renovations"	4) 90:6–42 Maccabean revolt and "a new house greater than the first one" (90:28–29)	4) --

This interpretation assumes that the history of *ApAb* ended before the last destruction of the Temple. There are no reliable data on the exact date of the document. Common opinion attributes it to the decades following the destruction of Jerusalem by the Romans (based on the description of the destruction of the Temple in 27:1–5). Nevertheless, according to the data of this verse as well as of 1:9 (possible reference to Caligula; see comm. to 1:9) and 27:1–7 (see comm. there) and the generally "templocentric" attitude of the document (cf. 1:2–3; 25:4; 27:1–5; 29:18), *ApAb* might have been composed, with at least equal probability, in the late Second Temple period.

1.3.7. CS гласъ *'voice' (15:7)*
Gk φωνή *here 'language'*

Having arrived to the heavens Abraham meets a terrifying "crowd of many people" (angels) who were "changing in appearance and likeness, running and being transformed and bowing *and shouting in a language the words of which I did not know* (и зъвуща гласомъ словесъ егоже не вѣдяхъ) (15:7) The italicized section was previously misinterpreted. Bonw: "und rufend mit einer Stimme der Worte, welche ich nicht kannte." The same in BL: "crying with a sound of words which I knew not." RL: "crying aloud words I did not know." Phil: "et clamaient d'une voix dont je ne connaissais pas les mots." Rub: "et se prosternant en criant des paroles, que je ne connaissais pas." The translation of Phil is closest to the correct one. Other are syntactically or semantically absurd, although some of them could be confirmed by the existence of the word combination "sound/voice of words"—Gk φωνή ῥημάτων—Heb קוֹל מִלִּין (Job 33:8; 34:16). However, the only way to reach a perfect reading of the verse is to consider that CS гласъ regularly renders Gk φωνή, meaning not only 'voice,' 'sound' (Heb קוֹל; cf. 16:3; 17:1 and LXX *pass.*) but also 'language' (Heb לָשׁוֹן; cf. LXX and MT in Isa 54:17). On the special language(s) of angels see *TestJob* 48:3, 49:2; 50:1, 2 ("angelic dialect(s)"); 1 Cor 13:1 ("tongues of angels"); cf. also Acts 2:11; 10:46.

1.3.8. CS сѣмо 'here' (16:1)
Gk ὧδε here 'thus; in this wise'

Frightened by his ascension to heaven Abraham asks the guiding angel Yahoel: камо (BSU како al.) мя нынѣ възведе сѣмо (16:1). Usually translated according to most of the mss: "How have you now brought me here?" This translation is not contextually perfect (see *Translation*). BL and RL render CS како 'how' by 'why,' considering, apparently, the double meaning of Gk πῶς 'how' and 'why' (cf. 20:7). Rub proposes an almost correct translation: "Où m'as tu fait monter" (Heb אנה העליתני), but ignores the word сѣмо 'here' contradicting his interpretation (since with сѣмо in its regular meaning the verse would look absurd: "Where have you now brought me here?"). The solution is in the fact that Gk adv. ὧδε, normally rendered by CS сѣмо, means both 'here' and 'thus; in this wise.'

1.3.9. CS когда 'when' (20:4)
Gk πότε here 'ever'

In 20:3 God asks Abraham: "Look from on high at the stars which are beneath you and count them for me and tell <me> their number!" And according to the Slavonic translation Abraham answers: "*When* shall I be able? [когда (+ когда S) возмогу] For I am [but] a man!" (cf. Gen 15). CS когда возмогу literally means "when shall I be able," which does not conform to the context. CS когда regularly reproducing Gk πότε 'when' must render here interrogative (εἴ) πότε reflecting Heb אִם(ה). Gen 15:5 in the same context has: (ה)תוכל אם "would you be able":

| And he [God] said: "Look at heaven and count the stars. *Would you be able* to count them?" And he [God] said to him [Abraham]: "So will be your seed!" (Gen 15:5) | <And he [God] said,> "Look from on high at the stars which are beneath you and count them for me and tell <me> their number!" And I [Abraham] said, *"Would I be able?* For I am [but] a man." And he said to me, "As the number of the stars and their host, so shall I make your seed into a company of nations (*ApAb* 20:3–5) |

1.3.10. CS древодѣля *'carpenter' (25:1)*
 Gk τέκτων *'carpenter,' 'craftsman'*
 Heb חרש *here 'smith,' also 'carpenter'*

In his heavenly vision Abraham "saw there the likeness of the idol of jealousy, as a likeness of a carpenter's [work] such as my father made, and its statue was of shining copper"—видѣхъ подобие идола ревнования яко подобие древодѣльско якоже дѣлаше оць мои и тѣло его мѣди льщащася (25:1). The verse is a combination of Ezek 8:5 (סמל הקנאה) "idol of jelousy") and 40:3 (according to LXX and similar to its Slavonic versions: ὡσεὶ ὅρασις χαλκοῦ στίλβοντος—видѣние мѣди льщащися (Srezn:2.69), while MT has only: כמראה נחשת "as a likeness of copper") or rather Dan 10:6: כעין נחשת קלל with the same Greek rendering as Ezek 40:3. However, there is a contradiction in the Slavonic text: the idol is described as a "carpenter's work," being at the same time "of shining copper." The solution is in the fact that the Greek *Vorlage* must have contained Gk τέκτων 'carpenter,' which usually rendered in LXX Heb חרש with a meaning much wider than 'carpenter' (generally 'workman'): the Hebrew word was reproduced also by Gk χαλκεύς '(copper-)smith' (2 Chr 24:12; Isa 54:16) among other Greek words (τεχνίτης, οἰκοδόμος, ἀρχιτέκτων, etc.; see Santos 1973:s.v.). The 𝔐 must contain: כמראה מלאכת/מעשה חרש; cf. Exod 35:35 or Jer 10:9; Hos 13:2, etc.

1.3.11. CS притещи *'come'* (27:3)
Gk κατατρέχω here *'descend'*

1.3.12. CS разъграбити *'plunder'* (27:3)
Gk (δι)αρπάζω here *'seize,' 'take'*

Two calques may occur in the description of the Temple destruction in 27:3: *се видѣхъ притекшая к нимъ съходы* (SU *въходы al.*) *четыри и црквь зажегоша огньмь и сущая в неи стая разграбиша*—"And behold, I saw four angels [or: "hosts"] *descending* to them [to the people on the right side of the visionary picture]. And they burned the temple with fire, and they *took* the holy things that were in it" (27:3). If we accept the suggestion of that the *hapax legomenon съхода* means 'angel' or 'host of angels' (see 1.2.5.; according to the motif of four angels burning the Temple attested in *2 Bar* 6:4–5; *Pesiqta Rabbati* 26,131; etc.), we have to assume that CS *притещи* here must mean rather 'descend' than 'come,' rendering Gk κατατρέχω, meaning not only 'come' but also 'descend' (see counterparts in *Greg. Naz.* 11th cent. 5—Srezn:2.479) and CS *разграбити* here and in 27:4 as well as *расхытити* (27:1,5) means here not 'plunder,' but like its regular Greek counterpart (δι)αρπάζω (Slov:3.565; Srezn:3.32), rather 'seize,' 'snatch,' 'carry away' (LSJ:245–246, 410). In later sources Gk (δι)αρπάζω may even mean simply 'take' "without idea of violence and injustice" (Lampe 1961:1.228–229). The latter meanings of the verb would be more appropriate to the context presumed by the preceding comments, positing that the subjects of action in the verse are "angels" and not "heathens." This interpretation also corresponds to the accounts of *2 Bar* 6:7; *4 Bar* 3; 2 Macc 2:4–8, etc., in which holy accessories of the destroyed Temple were carried away by angels. Thus, the verse as a whole would appear thus:

καὶ εἶδον τέσσαρα συναγωγὰς [or: τέσσαρας πρέσβεις] κατατρέχοντας πρὸς αὐτοὺς καὶ ἐνέπρεσαν τὸν ναὸν ἐν πυρὶ καὶ ἥρπασαν τὰ ἐν αὐτῷ ὄντα ἅγια

וארא את ארבעה המחנות [א׳: המלאכים] יורדים עליהם ויבעירו את המקדש ואת הקדשים אשר בו חטפו

with the following counterparts:

CS *съходъ*[9]   Gk πρέσβυς   Heb מלאך

---

[9] See 1.2.5.

or | or
CS *съхода* | Gk συναγωγή | Heb מחנה or קהל
CS *притещи* | Gk κατατρέχω | Heb ירד or נחת
CS *разграбити* | Gk (δι)αρπάζω | Heb תפס or חטף

1.3.13. CS ослаба *'relaxing' (29:8)*
Gk ἄνεσις *here 'willfulness'*

Chapter 29, where a messianic (or anti-messianic) figure is introduced, is the most enigmatic in the entire writing. CS *ослаба* of 29:8 is a key definition of this messianic figure: "Hear, Abraham, the man whom you saw shamed and struck and again worshiped is the *ослаба* of the heathen for the people who will come from you in the last days." Previous interpretations of the word were conditioned by the understanding of most of the chapter as a Christian interpolation, and the figure introduced in it as Jesus (although he is "going out from the left side of the heathen," kissed by Azazel, etc., see below). Cf. BL: "relief" (Gk ἄνεσις, Heb מנוחה), Phil: "soulagera," Rub: "délivrance" (Gk ἄνεσις, ἔνδοσις, ἄδεια), RL: "liberation." Actually, Greek counterparts of CS *ослаба, ослабление, ослабѣние* may also have negative connotations: "willfulness"—Gk ἄνεσις or "weakening," "laxity"—Gk ἔκλυσις, παράλυσις (Mikl: 518; Srezn: 2.723–724; SRJa11–17: 13.1013). The last one might have rendered Heb רפיון and relate to a pseudo-Messiah; cf. רפיון התורה "laxity [= neglect] of the Law" (*Lam. Rab.* 1,4) or רפיון ידים מן התורה "laxity of hands in upholding the Law" (*Midrash Tanhuma, Beshalah* 25). Cf. also חולש על גוים of Isa 14:12 similar to *ослаба отъ* (om. KO) *языкъ* here.

We suppose that the eschatological scenario of *ApAb* 29 might have the well known Jewish eschatological duo-messianic structure (in this case: anti-Messiah vs. true Messiah). This assumption helps to remove contradictions in the description of the messianic figure: in 29:4–8 the text speaks of an anti-Messiah (known as Beliar/Belial, Malqi-Resh'a of the pseudepigrapha and Qumran documents or Armilus of Targum Isa 11:4 and later Jewish sources, Antichrist of NT; see, e.g., Milik 1972; Schürer 1973:2.526,553–554; 3.336n, 450) "going out from the left side of the heathen" and "worshiped by the heathen with Azazel":

<And I looked> and saw a man going out from the left side of the heathen. Men and women and children, great crowds, went out from the side of the heathen and they worshiped him. <And> while I was still looking, those on the right side went out, and some shamed this man,[10] and some struck him, and

---

[10] CS *срамяхуся* (SA *срамляху* BDIKO). The oldest mss have a reflexive form, which probably reproduced either Gk ἐντρέπομαι (Srezn 3.476, 478) meaning 'be ashamed' as well as 'turn toward,' 'reverence' (cf. Mark 12:6; LXX Lev 26:41 rendering Heb כנע here

some worshiped him. <And> I saw that as they worshiped him, Azazel ran and worshiped, and having kissed his face he turned and stood behind him. And I said, "Eternal Mighty One! Who is this shamed and struck man, worshiped by the heathen with Azazel?" And he answered and said, "Hear, Abraham, the man whom you saw shamed and struck and again worshiped is the *laxity* of the heathen for the people who will come from you in the last days, in this twelfth hour of the age of impiety.

However, in 29:9 and in the first clause of 29:10 the true Messiah "from the seed of Abraham" is meant:

And in the [same] twelfth period of the close of my age[11] I shall set up the man from your seed which you saw. Everyone from my people will [finally] admit him, while the sayings of him who was as if called by me will be neglected in their minds.[12]

'humble oneself') or less probably Gk αἰσχύνομαι 'be ashamed, dishonored' (Srezn 3.476, 478).

[11] CS *вѣка моего скончания*. Usually understood as "of my final age" (lit: "age of my end") or as "age of my fulfillment." The same inversion occurs in 25:6: *суда коньчания* "of the close of the judgment." Cf. *Ostr* Matt 13:40: *съконьчание вѣка сего*—ἐν τῇ συντελείᾳ τοῦ αἰῶνος τούτου; cf. *ApAb* 29:3: *до скончания времени* "until the end of the time" (עד קץ הימים (?); cf. Dan 12:13). Since CS *вѣкъ* may render also Gk καιρός, Heb עת or מועד meaning 'time, term,' then Gk συντελεία/πέρας καιροῦ "end of the time" rendering Heb עת הקץ "time of the end" (Dan 11:35, 40, 12:4, 9) is also possible (in this case *суда коньчания* in 25:6 may go back to the unattested Heb משפט הקץ "the judgment of the end").

[12] The second clause of this verse is very vague and probably corrupt: *изъ* (om. S) *людии моихъ сему вси уподобятся и притъчи яко отъ мене зовома преминующеся въ свѣтехъ своихъ*. The first words *изъ* (om. S) *людии моихъ* "from my people" were usually attached to the previous sentence, while the rest of the verse was translated as follows: "… diesem werden alle nachahmen und hinzugezält werden wie von mir gerufen, die sich ändernden in ihren Ratschlüssen" (Bonw); "this one all will follow, and such as called by me (will) join, (even) those who change in their counsels" (BL); "Celui-là, tous le suivront. Et ajoute ceux qui auront changé dans leur conseil, parce qu'ils auront été appelés par Moi" (Phil); "All will imitate him … (you) consider [*притъчи* as imperative from *притъкнути*] him as one called by me … (they) are changed [*прѣмѣнующеся*] in their counsels" (RL). Our reading is not more than an alternative interpretation, although based on the new understanding of the whole chapter (see comm. to 29:8): the verse speaks of two persons: one is "the man from your [Abraham's] seed," the true Messiah of the previous verse, while "he who was as if called by me" is the Pseudo-Messiah of 29:4–8, 11–13. Then, CS *уподобятся* might have rendered Gk ὁμολογέω 'acknowledge, admit, confess' (confused here with ὁμοιόω?) used also with dat. (cf. concerning Jesus in Matt 10:32) or Gk νομοθετέω (see Srezn:3.1240) in *pass*. 'ordained by law' (cf. Heb 8:6). Both Gk words rendered Heb ידה in *hiph'il* 'confess, acknowledge' (see LXX for Job 40:14(10); Aq Th Ps 99(98):3 and Prov 28:13, etc.). CS *преминующеся* here in previous research was always emended to *прѣмѣнущеся* 'change(d).' In the light of the interpretation introduced above the emendation is not

For other doubts concerning Christian interpolations in *ApAb* see Licht (1971) and Hall (1988).

1.3.14. CS утврьдити *'sustain' (29:18)*
Gk στηρίζω *'sustain' also with food*
Heb סעד *'sustain with food'*

After the ten plagues will have been brought "upon all earthly creation," only the righteous men from the seed of Abraham will be left "kept by Me by number, hastening in the glory of My name to the place prepared beforehand for them" (29:15–17). The will live "being *affirmed* by the sacrifices and the offerings of justice and truth in the age of justice" (*утверждаеми жертвами и даръми правды и* (om. S) *истины*) (29:18). CS *утврьдити* most probably renders its regular Gk equivalent στηρίζω, reflecting here Heb סעד 'sustain with food' (Judg 19:5,8; Ps 104(105):15; etc.), while "the gifts of justice"— unattested Heb מנחות צדק (?) "offerings of justice"—resembles זבחי צדק "sacrifices of justice" (in LXX always in sg.: θυσία δικαιοσύνης; see Deut 33:19; Pss 4:6(5); 51:21(19)). CS *даръ* renders Gk δῶρον, Heb מנחה "offering" also in 13:3 (see comm. *ibid.*). This means that "the righteous men" will feed on the sacrifices like priests. This interpretation goes well with other manifestations of the special importance of the Temple and sacrifices for the author of *ApAb* (cf. 1:2–3; 9:9; 25:4; 27:1–7).

1.3.15. CS владыка *'ruler' (30:6)*
Gk ἐξουσία here *'domain' (Heb מדינה)*

The fifth plague brought upon the nations will be *въ владыкахъ ихъ орениемъ труса и меча гыбель* (30:6). It is usually translated: "destruction *among their rulers* through the ravage of earthquake and sword," according to the most widespread meaning of CS *владыка* rendering Gk δεσπότης, ἡγεμών (Mikl:66; Srezn:1.267). In this case the earthquake would have killed selectively—only the "rulers." The word refers rather to Gk ἐξουσία 'power,' 'authority' as it did in *Ostr* Matt 8:9 (*подъ владыкою*—ὑπὸ ἐξουσίαν "under authority"). We propose the translation based on another meaning of Gk ἐξουσία—'domain, district' (cf., e.g., LXX for Dan 3:2, where this Greek word renders Aram מדינתא). Thus, "their domains" of the fifth plague is parallel to

---

necessary: CS *прѣминути(ся)* rendered Gk παρατρέχω meaning here 'neglect,' 'deliberately overlook' or Gk ὑπερβαίνω 'trespass,' are both appropriate to the context (Slov:3.458; Mikl:736; Srezn:2.1666; cf. Lampe:1027). CS *с(ъ)вѣтъ* reproduces Gk βουλή, Heb עצה, דעת, מחשבה in 22:2; 23:10; 23:14; 26:5.

"their native land" of the previous plague in 30:5 ("the fourth [plague] is famine in their native land").[13]

1.3.16. CS како 'how' (20:7)
Gk πῶς here 'why'

The visionary asks God: *како ... утвердися с нимъ* (*ними* SD). Lit. "How ... have you set yourself with him [Azazel]?" or "How ... has it been set with him? [or: them SD]." CS *како*, usually rendering Gk πῶς meaning both 'how' and 'why,' was always translated as 'how' here according to its most widespread meaning in CS (cf. comm. to 16:1). Thus, the whole verse looked obscure to the commentators (see, e.g., RL:699, n. 20h). It was mistakenly recognized as a Gnostic or Bogomilian interpolation reflecting a dualistic world outlook (see RL:684). Proper understanding of Abraham's first question to God helps to clarify the nature of this verse, as does the content of the further vision (chapters 21–23), which presents the answer to this question: having been ascertained that there is only "one power" in Heaven (the dualistic doctrine of "two powers," שתי רשויות, is frequently alluded to in rabbinic literature; cf. *b. Haggiga* 15a, *Gen. Rab.* 1; *EccR* 2,12, etc.) Abraham wonders at the existence of Azazel in the world, since this "power" has no part in Heaven ("while he is now not before you"), i.e., it is the question of the existence of evil in the monotheistic world.

Semantic calques occur also in the examples discussed in other chapters:

CS *даръ* 'gift'—Gk δῶρον here 'offering' (Heb מנחה) (13:2)
CS *с(ъ)вѣтъ* 'counsel'—Gk βουλή 'will,' 'reason,' 'design' (22:2; 23:10; 23:14; 26:5,6 29:10)

---

[13] "Their native land"—*уселеныя рода ихъ*. Lit. "the inhabited world of their kin"—Gk τῆς οἰκουμένης (or: γῆς) τοῦ γένεος (or: τῆς γενέσεως, or: πατρίδος) αὐτῶν Hebrew ארץ מולדתם "their native land"; cf. Gen 31:13; Ruth 2:11; Jer 22:10; Ezek 23:15, etc.

1.4. Syntactic Hellenisms

1.4.1. CS тьзъ + *gen. (10:3)*
Gk ἐπώνυμος + *gen. "name-sake of"*

In 10:3 the protagonist hears "the voice of the Holy One" saying: *иди иаоилъ тъже* (S *аль тезе* A *яѡль тезе* B *яѡл тьзе* K *доль тезе* D *аоильзе* I *ангеле* C) *посредѣстьва* (S *посредиества* A *посредства* B) *неизрекомаго имени моего* (A—my word division, Tikhonravov proposes: *альтезе*; K—my word division, Porfir'ev: *идия ѡльтьзе*). CS *тьзъ* (*тьзь, тезъ, тозъ*) regularly renders Gk ἐπώνυμος + gen. or -νυμος after another root (cf. Lunt 1985:59–60). Normally used with dat.; cf. *неистовьству тьзъ, бгословию тезъ, тезъ ѡму* (Srezn:2.1078). Its Greek counterpart, however, demands gen., as it is in our case—*посредѣстьва*. Therefore, Slavonic prototext *иди иаоилъ тьзъ посрѣдъства неизрекомаго имени моего* may be retroverted to Gk ἦλθε Ἰαοὴλ ὁ ἐπώνυμος τοῦ μεσίτου τοῦ ἀφάτου νόμου μου—"Go, Yahoel, the namesake of the mediation of my ineffable name." This interpretation corresponds to the meaning of Heb יואל/יהואל, which is a combination of God's names. See *b.Sanhedrin* 38b: זהו מטטרון ששמו כשם רבו "This is Metatron whose name is like that of his Master" (leaning on "I send an angel ... my name is in him" of Exod 23:20–21). Yahoel and Metatron, whose functions are very similar, are explicitly identified in *3 En* 48D:1 (cf. Scholem 1946:68–70).[14]

---

[14] Cf. 10:8: *азъ есмь иаоилъ ... сила посредѣ е[с]мь неизъглаголемаго слежаща имене въ мнѣ*, which probably means: "I am Yahoel... I am a power in the midst of the Ineffable who put together his names in me." CS *посредѣемь* SU *посредесмь* C *посредиемъ al.* (translated here as "I am ... in the midst of ...") was usually understood as inst. sg. "through the medium." Mss SCU, however, witness another reading: *посредѣемь* < *посредѣ еᶜмь* (SU) and *посредесмь* < *посред[ъ] есмь* (C). Cf. *посредствьо* in our verse (10:3). We reconstruct either Gk (ἐγώ) εἰμι ... ὁ ἐν (τῷ) μέσῳ ..., Heb אנ(וכ)י בקרב "I am ... in the midst of ..." (see HR:461–467) or more probably Gk (ἐγώ) εἰμι ... ὁ μεσίτης. The words in 10:8 and 10:3 might render Gk μέσος, μεσότης 'middle, mediation' (cf. Mikl:638: *посрѣдие*—μεσότης). For 10:3 Gk μεσίτης 'mediator' is also probable, especially in light of the parallels: *TDan* 6:2: τῷ ἀγγέλῳ τῷ παραιτουμένῳ ὑμᾶς ὅτι οὗτός ἐστι μεσίτης θεοῦ καὶ ἀνθρώπων "to the angel who intercedes for you, for he is the mediator between God and men," cf. *TLev* 5:6: ἐγώ εἰμι ὁ ἄγγελος ὁ παραιτούμενος." For μεσίτης denoting a mediator between God and men see also Job 9:33 (Heb מוכיח); Gal 3:19–20; 1 Tim 2:5; Heb 9:15. On Metatron in this role see Odeberg (1928:103–104). Some scholars derived the very name of Metatron from Lat *mediator* (see Odeberg 1928:135).

Cf. also *неизрекомаго имени* "ineffable name" of 10:3 and *неизъглаголемаго* S *изъглаголемаго al.* 'ineffable' here. The variant of S *неизъглаголемаго* 'ineffable' (and not *изъглаголемаго* 'said,' 'uttered' of other mss) seems to be more plausible in this

1.4.2. CS творити власть + на + acc. (14:3)
        Gk ἐξουσιάζω + ἐπί + acc. 'have power over s.-o.'

During the offering on mount Horeb, Azazel tries to seduce Abraham, and the guiding angel Yahoel begins his instructions of how Abraham can protect himself from Azazel with the following words: *дерзаи и твори* (*створи* A) *власть сию* (CKO *властию* ABDI) *еликоже азъ заповедаю тебѣ на укоряющаго* (*укоряющая* A) *правду* (14:3). The reading of ABDI—*створи властию*—might have been reconstructed as ποίει ἐν ἐξουσίᾳ "do with authority" (well attested in NT; cf. Matt 21:24; Mark 11:28,29; Luke 20:2, etc., rendered usually by *творити властию* in Slavonic versions of Gospels). However, in this case, (1) the sentence as a whole seems to be incomplete, and (2) ms A elsewhere in this passage reflects a secondary version: *тебе* for *тя* (14:2), *укоряющая* for *укоряющаго* (14:3) *вѣщавша* for *свѣщавша* (14:4; cf. Rubinstein 1953:109). The reading of CKO—*твори* (*створи* A) *власть*—without being emended, and with *власть* understood as Gk ἀρχή, κράτος or ἐξουσία, remains obscure. The only way to interpret the text is to assume that the reading reflected in CKO—*твори* (*створи* A) *власть* {*сию*}—is a calque of Gk ἐξουσιάζω 'have power,' built according to the very common model: verb + abstract noun in acc. without preposition reproducing a single Greek word (see Копыленко 1973:147–148; Moczyński 1975:257–259); cf., e.g., CS *напасти творити* for Gk διώκω (*Zogr* Matt 5:44), CS *сътворити скръбь* and *печаль творити* for Gk θλίβειν (Istrin:1.336,6;116,13; Копыленко 1973:147). This reconstruction may be confirmed by the fact that Gk ἐξουσιάζω could be used with the prep. ἐπί (CS *на*) + acc.: 'have power over s.-o.'; cf. ἐξουσιάζονται ἐπὶ τὸν λαόν (Neh 5:15). Thus, we have *твори*

---

context. Nevertheless, the reading of most mss may go back to Heb שם המפורש "Explicit [lit. 'expressed clearly'] Name' denoting actually the same *nomen ineffabile* (Tetragrammaton) in its explicit form; cf. the use of this term in *3 En* 22:5,48B,D:5.

Our intrpretation of 10:3 helps to clarify also the meaning of the following segment here: *слежаща* (*слежаще* B) *имене* (*имени* KO) *въ мнѣ*. The verse as a whole was always understood as "I am Yahoel… a power through the medium of his *ineffable name dwelling* in me." Srezn also posits the meanings 'пребывать, находится' ad loc. (3.731). However, the placing of *слежаща* 'dwelling' in the sentence—whether it relates to *имене/имени* 'name(s)' or to *сила* 'power'—requires justification. We propose to treat here *сълежати* as 'lay/put together,' according to its rarer meaning attested in *Io. ex.* 76 (Srezn:3.731, s.v. *сълежатися*), used in the prototext with acc. pl. *имени* (as in mss KO) and not with gen. sg. or nom. pl. *имене*. This interpretation goes well with the meaning of the Heb equivalent of CS *иаоилъ*—יהואל/יואל which is a combination of God's names (see 10:3). Cf. *3 En* 48D:5: אלו ע' שמות מעין שם המפורש ... שנטל הקב"ה משמו המפורש והניחם על שמו של מטטרון "These 70 names (are) a reflection of the Explicit Name … which the Holy One, blessed be He, took from his Explicit Name and put upon the name of Metatron."

власть ... на укоряющаго правду "have power ... over him who reviles justice." And the whole verse will be: "Be bold and have power, as I order you, over him who reviles justice."[15]

1.4.3. CS гнѣватися + *dat. (23:14)*
Gk χολόω/ὀργίζω + dat. *"be angry"*

Abraham wonders: "Eternal Mighty One! Why did you will to do so that evil is desired in the heart of man?" and then explains his question by the very obscure (in Slavonic) argument: *зане гнѣваешися на изволеное тебѣ* (*твое* AC) *въ свѣтѣ твоемъ* (*нъ свѣть ствоемь* S) *дѣлающему неполезное*—"Since you are angry at what was willed by you, who does a bad thing[16] according to your design"[17] (23:14). Unusual dat. *дѣлающему* after *гнѣватися* may be a syntactic calque: both Gk χολόω and ὀργίζω 'be angry' are used with object in dat.

---

[15] In order to demonstrate the whole range of possible interpretations (although of different grade of probability), we shall list also some possible emendations. (1) CS *творити власть* might have gone back to the corrupted *творити влашта* < Gk σφετερίζομαι 'appropriate' (Slov:1.201; Mikl:68; Srezn:1.275), relating to the heavenly garment from the last verse of the previous chapter (13:14: "The garment which in heaven was formerly yours [belonging to the fallen angel—Azazel] has been set aside for him [Abraham], and the corruption which was on him has gone over to you."). However, this idea that does not appear convincing. (2) It may be posited that *твори власть сию* and (*с*)*твори властию* go back to *) *твори съ властию сею* of the fore-text, while *власть* reproduces ἀρχή or ἐξουσία: "do with this Power." "Power" may relate to Azazel: both Gk words are widely attested in the meaning of 'heavenly powers' or even 'powers of evil,' 'demonic powers' (Rom 8:38; Eph 6:12; 1 Pet 3:22, etc.; Lampe:236,502); cf. Slov:1.200; SDRJa11–14:1.446). (3) CS *власть* is also attested rendering Gk ἄδεια, meaning there 'power' (Istrin 1920–1922:1.223,22) and 'license' (Srezn:1.273). Thus, *твори власть си{ю}* may go back to the Gk idiom ἄδειαν ποιεῖσθαι or ἄδειαν ποιεῖν σοί "to secure oneself" (lit. "make power to o.-self"; LSJ:20; Dvoretskij:1.31). The angel says: "Secure yourself as I order you," meaning the order in 14:12: "Whatever he says to you, answer him not, lest his will run up to you. For God gave him the gravity and the will against those who answer him. Answer him not."

[16] Lit. "useless thing." CS *неполезное* rendering Gk ἄχρηστος, ἀχρεῖος, lit. 'useless,' may mean also 'bad, evil.' Its Gk counterparts reproduce Heb אין-חפץ 'undesirable' (Hos 8:8) and שפל 'base' (2 Sam 6:22).

[17] CS *въ свѣтѣ твоемъ* must go back to Heb בעצתך or בדעתך (on CS *с(ъ)вѣтъ* understood as Gk βουλή, Heb עצה or דעת; cf. 22:2; 23:10; 26:5–6; 29:10). Another possibility is that *нъ свѣть ствоемь* (S) and *въ свѣтѣ твоемъ* (*al.*) reflect a fore-text (*нъ*) *въ свѣтѣ своемъ* "(but) according to its own reason": "you are angry at what was willed by you, (but) [which is] doing a bad thing according to its own reason/will" (according to the idea of 26:5).

1.4.4.   CS всяко яко *(26:4)*
         Gk πάντως ὅτι *"evidently because"*

In the course of discussion presenting the idea of the freedom of will (cf. comm. to the same verse below), God asks Abraham: "Why did your father Terah not listen to your voice and abandon the demonic idolatry until he perished, and all his house with him?" And Abraham answers: превѣчне крѣпче всяко яко неволися ему слушати мене ни азъ же послѣдовахъ дѣломъ его— "Eternal <Mighty One>! Evidently because he did not will to listen to me, nor did I follow his deeds" (26:4). CS *всяко яко* is translated here as "evidently because," since the most appropriate Greek equivalent here would be πάντως ὅτι; see, e.g., Damascius, *De Principiis*, 96 (LSJ:1031).

See also syntactic Hellenisms mentioned in other chapters:

CS *готовъ бываетъ*—Gk ἕτοιμόν ἐστιν "inevitable" (26:5)
CS *срѣсти* + dat.)—Gk (ἀπ-/ὑπ-)συναντάω + dat. 'meet' (27:10)
CS *отъ нихъ* "from them"—Gk ἐκ τούτων "since then" (27:11)

1.5. Phraseological Hellenisms

1.5.1.   CS принести цѣну *"bring a price" (4:2)*
         Gk τιμὴν φέρειν *"give honor"*

In 4:2 Terah praises Abraham блгслвнъ ты аврааме бмъ (бгъ богомъ B) моимъ зане принесе цѣну (цѣны SU) бъвъ, lit."Blessed by my god [or: "to my gods"] are you, Abraham, for you brought the price of the gods."[18] The first part of the verse contains a syntactic biblicism which we shall discuss below. More problematic is the second part: принесе цѣну (цѣны SU) бъвъ. The solution is in the fact that Gk τιμὴν φέρειν—which may be restored from CS принести цѣну—means not only "bring the price" but also "give honor" (LSJ:1793), while τιμὴ θεῶν "the honor to gods" is also well attested (*ibid.*). The word 'price' might have looked appropriate to Slav translator, since the dialogue follows the episode where Abraham has succesfully sold some idols from his father's workshop.

---

[18] Mss SU (*цѣны*) have either acc. pl. or a rare example of a direct object in gen. with the verb *приносити*; cf. *принеси пръста твоего* in *Mar* John 20:27 (Vaillant 1948:#120); cf. also the use of the direct object in gen. with the verb *приносити* in 1:8: *принеси ми сѣчива и измала*.

The Greek *Vorlage* might also contain the same word-play as in the apocryphal *Gospel of Peter* 3, where it "may be a play on the double sense of τιμή ... the multitude are described as scourging Jesus and saying ταύτῃ τῇ τιμῇ τιμήσωμεν τὸν υἱον τοῦ θεοῦ 'with this honor let us honor' or 'at this price let us apprise the son of God'" (Moulton, Milligan 1930:635).

1.5.2.   *CS* сътворити свѣтъ *(5:8)*
         Gk φῶς ποιεῖν *"kindle fire"*

Having experienced the weakness of helplessly damaged idols (ch. 1–2), Abraham performs a final test, this time intentional, of one of them:

And it came to pass, after I had put the splinters on the fire, in order to cook food for my father, that I went out to ask about the food and I put [the idol] Bar-Eshath ["fiery"][19] near the hearth of fire, saying to him menacingly, "Bar-Eshath, make sure that the fire does not go out before I come back. If the fire does go out, blow on it to make it flare up." *[And] I went out, having kindled my fire.* When I came back again I found Bar-Eshath fallen backwards, his feet enveloped in fire and terribly burned. Laughing greatly to myself, I said, "Bar-Eshath, you certainly are able to kindle fire and cook food!" (5:6–9).

The problem is a passage translated here as "I went out, having made my fire" (*изидо*^{x} (АКО + *и al.*) *створи*^{x} *свѣ*^{m} *свои*). BL translate *створихъ свѣтъ* as "accomplished my purpose" and comment: "lit. 'did my counsel': a Hebrew phrase, עשה עצה 'execute a plan' (Isa 30:1)." This interpretation was accepted by all the later translators and commentators. Actually, this Hebrew idiom is attested only twice, in Isa 30:1 and Ps 13:3, where it means rather "plan" than "execute a plan." The following interpretation seems to be more appropriate. Mss АКО omit a conjunction *и* between the two verbs. The absence of *и* makes it syntactically possible to reconstruct a form **створи*^{в} in place of *створи*^{x} where the superscript *в* was altered by scribal error to *x* (cf. the alternation of *прѣмыслихъ* and *прѣмысливъ* in 5:1). Thus, the translation should be: "I went out, having made my fire," considering that CS *свѣтъ* renders here Gk φῶς meaning not only 'light' but also 'fire' (see, e.g., in Mark 14:54 and Luke 22:56; for φῶς ποιεῖν as 'kindle fire'; see, e.g., Xenophon, *Historia Graeca* 6, 2; LSJ:1916).

1.5.3.   *CS* народу народъ *(15:6)*
         Gk λαόν ὄχλῳ *"people in [great] numbers"*

---

[19] See comm. to 5:5.

or
Gk ὄχλος λαῶν *"crowd of people"*

On the night the visionary ascended with Yahoel he saw "a strong light which cannot be described" (15:5). And then an obscure description follows: *и се въ свѣтѣ томъ разъгнѣщенъ огнь народу* (+ *и* SU) *народъ многъ мужьска образа*. Cf. 18:13: "an indescribable light surrounded the fiery people" (*свѣтъ нескажаемъ объстояше народа огньнаго*) and *2 En* 1(A):5: "fireborn heavenly armies" (*огнероденъ вои небесныхъ*); cf. also *2 En* 29(J):3: "the ranks of the bodiless army created from fire." For angels made of fire see also *2 Bar* 21:6; *Pesiqta Rabbati* 33:10; *Sefer ha-Razim* 6:3–8, etc. (cf. Ps 104:4).

Some possible interpretations: (1) Lunt (1985:56) proposes the word division *огньна роду* "of fiery kin" (Lunt: "of fiery Gehenna," since CS *родъ* is attested rendering Gk γέεννα, confused with γενέα) in place of *огнь народу*. This reading is syntactically (and if to accept Lunt's interpretation, also contextually) implausible. (2) The first *народу* usually understood as dat. possesivus may render Gk dat. ὄχλῳ meaning 'in numbers' (cf., e.g., Xenophon, *Cyropaedia* 1.80; LSJ:s.v.). Thus, the whole verse would look like this: "And behold, in this light a fire was kindled, [and there were] a lot of people of male likeness in great numbers." (3) The second *народъ* usually understood as nom. sg. may be also interpreted as gen. pl. Two CS *народъ* may reproduce two different Greek words here: λαός and ὄχλος. Cf. a Greek phrase almost identical to our verse: ὁ πολύς λαῶν ὄχλος "the great crowd of people" (Aristophanes, *Ranae* 676). The last retroversion seems to be the most convincing: "And behold, in this light a fire was kindled [and there was] a crowd of many people in male likeness."

For phraseological Hellenisms see also:

CS *творити власть си* lit. "do power to oneself"—Gk ἄδειαν ποιεῖν σοί "secure oneself" (14:3n.)

CS *принести куплю* + dat. "bring a purchase"—Gk παρέχειν πρᾶγμα τινί "cause trouble to s.-o." (2:8)

Chapter 2
Semitic Original

The features of the Semitic original—and among them those which can hardly be common for Judaeo-Greek idiom—have been preserved even at the Slavonic stage of transmission of *ApAb*. The abundance of obvious Semitisms, and specifically Hebraisms, attested in the text of the document even led some scholars to raise the possibility of direct Slavonic translation from Hebrew (Rub:35–37). Arguments of varying cogency in favor of the Semitic original of our text were collected by Rubinstein (1953; 1954; 1957), Rubinkiewicz (1980; Rub:33–34) and Philinenko (Phil:23–24); many Semitisms are also adduced in the notes to the editions and translations of the document, mainly those by Box and Landsman (BL), Philonenko-Sayar and Philonenko (Phil), and Rubinkiewicz (Rub). On this stage, the existence of the Semitic original of *ApAb* may be considered proven beyond any doubt, since (1) the literal renderings of Hebrew or Aramaic are attested on different linguistic levels, and (2) the retroversion of Semitic forms helps to clarify difficulties of the Slavonic text.

2.1. Hebrew or Aramaic?

While the Semitic origin of the document might be considered proven, the problem of choice between *interpretatio hebraica* or *aramaica* cannot be solved unequivocally. In the period under discussion elements of these languages could be mixed in a single text. The only obvious Aramaic forms that we observe in our text are Aramaic proper names:

2.1.1. *CS* Марумафъ *(1:3,7; 3:8;* Марумафа *1:9;* Маруматъ *3:5)*
Aram (א)מר אומת *"the lord of the nation"*
(Gk *Μαρουμαθ(α)/Μαρουματ)*

In 1:3 Abraham, "having entered the temple for the service, has found a god named *Marumaf*, carved out of stone, fallen at the feet of an iron god, *Nakhon*"—*... въшедъ въ церковь ихъ на служение обретохъ бога Марумафа* (according to 1:3, 7; 3:8; *Марумафа* in 1:9, *Маруматъ* in 3:5) *именемъ отъ камени извая́на падша ницъ у ногу бога нахона* A *нарицена* S *нахина al.*) *желѣзнаго.* A stone idol, like Dagon in 1 Sam 5:3–4, is found prostrate in his sanctuary, and after an attempt to put him back his head breaks off. Rubinkiewicz believes that "Maroumat is an abbreviation of the Hebrew *Martā Rômā*" (RL). Box posits here אבן מרמה "'stone of deceit,' which was a chief object of Abraham's worship at this period" (BL; cf. Phil: "de l'hébreu *miremoth* 'tromperies')." Developing the idea of Box we could add that מרמה is well attested in MT in the pl.—מרמות (which is more close phonetically to *марумат/фъ*), and that a homographic name of Jewish priests מרמות occurs in Ezra 8:33; 10:36; Neh 3:4,21; 10:6; 12:3. In LXX it is transliterated either as Μαρειμωθ (L, Neh 12:3) or Μαρεμωθ (A, Ezra 10:36). In Ps 36:4 מרמה is used together with און, whereas *ApAb* 6:9 contains another name of an idol— *иоавонъ*—probably going back to און (see comm. *ibid.*). Thus, י(ו)און and אל מרמות in *ApAb* might have been parallel to און ומרמה of Ps 36:4.

We prefer, nevertheless, to reject this etymology, reconstructing here Gk *Μαρουμαθα/Μαρουματ, which unambiguously follows from the Slavonic transliteration, reproducing the Aram מר אומת(א) "the lord of the nation(s)" (Jastrow 1903:26–27; Sokoloff 1990:44). There are other Semitic names of deities derived according to the same model: Aram *mr ylhy* "lord of gods" and Akk *mr byty* "lord of house" (Green 1992:67; *DDD*:1370).

In our story, when the head of the idol breaks off, Terah puts the head of another idol on the body of the broken one; vv. 3:6–8 define Mar-Umath as the idol "having the head of one stone and being made of another stone" (*марумафъ богъ отца моего другаго камыка главу имы и отъ другаго камыка сътворенъ*). This brings to mind a Roman custom of changing the heads of emperor's statues. Suetonius ascribes to Caligula this kind of mass alteration of Greek statues of gods: "… he began from that time on *to claim to divine majesty*; for after giving orders that such statues of the gods as were especially famous for their sanctity or their artistic merit, including that of Jupiter of Olympia, should be brought from Greece, in order *to remove their heads and put his own in their place…*" (Suetonius, *De Vita Caesarum* 4 (Cal.), 22; italics added). Images of Caligula were introduced in the Alexandrian synagogues (Philo, *Leg.* 20, 25, 29, 30), and he was also the first to try to bring the emperor's cult to Jerusalem, ordering his statue to be set up in the Temple. Thus, the very name מר אומת(א) may go back to Gk κύριος ἔθνους or Lat *dominus populi*, designating an idolized Roman emperor, most probably Caligula (for Roman emperor called κύριος, equivalent of Lat *dominus*, see, e.g., Acts 25:26). Negative accounts of Caligula in other Jewish sources from the same period are found in *Syb. Or.* 12:50–67 and possibly in 3 Macc 2:22, where the idolized Ptolemy, very likely identified in this composition with Caligula (they both claimed divine honors and tried to defile the Jerusalem Temple), also falls, having entered the Temple. In any case, the tradition of the fall (= disgrace) of an idol or an idolized figure is much older; cf. the same sequence of events in *ApAb* 1:3, 6 and 1 Sam 5:3–4: Mar-Umath and the Phoenician god Dagon are both found fallen in their own sanctuaries and, after an attempt to set them up again, their heads (in the case of Dagon, also his hands) are found broken off.

Semitic Original 63

2.1.2. CS Варисатъ *(5:5,6,9,10,14,17; 6:9,10)*
  Aram (א)בר אשת *'fiery' (Gk* *Βαρησατ/θ(α))

Another Aramaic name occurs in 5:5. There is an idol named in CS *Варисатъ*; it obviously renders Aram (א)בר אשת (Gk *Βαρησατ/θ(α)) 'fiery' (lit. 'the son of fire'; first noticed by Ginzberg 1906). We can add that the similar name *yšt* is attested for the Ugaritic goddess of fire (Dietrich, Loretz, Sanmartín 1976; *DDD*:626–627), Philo of Alexandria in his *Phoenician History* (according to Eusebius, *Praeparationis Evangelicae* 1.10,9) also lists three Phoenician gods of fire, translating their names into Greek as Φως, Πυρ and Φλοξ. The "Fiery" is quite appropriate to the function of this idol in the story: having been made of wood, he maintains the fire but eventually is burned by it.

However, Aramaic proper names co-exist with Hebrew ones:

2.1.3. CS Нахон *(1:3)*
  Heb נכון *'stable; firmly established' (Gk* Ναχων)

In 1:3, Mar-Umath is found fallen at the feet of an iron god, *Nakhon*. According to ms A, it is *Нахонъ*; ms S has an emendation *нарицена*, other mss contain a form *Нахинъ*. The reading of A should be preferred: Heb נכון 'stable; firmly established'—a "speaking name" like other idol names in this text—is used to emphasize that this idol has not fallen, in contrast to Mar-Umath. Cf. פסל לא ימוט "sculpture which will not fall" (Isa 40:20) and יחזקום ולוא יפיק "they [= idol-makers] fasten it [= idol] that it will not move" (Jer 10:4).

The same form of a proper name—נכון (LXX: Ναχων)—occurs in 2 Sam 6:6, where the ark of God is going to fall before גרן נכון "threshing-floor of Nakhon." Heb גרן 'threshing-floor,' or sometimes generally 'open place' (as in 1 Kgs 22:10; 1 Chr 18:9), is associated with a sacred place, place of worship in 2 Sam 24:18; 1 Chr 21:18, 28; 2 Chr 3:1, where it designates a location of David's altar and Solomon's Temple (גרן ארונה/ארנן היבוסי).

***

As well as the proper names, most Semitic forms in our document may reflect an Aramaic original as well as a Hebrew one. In very rare cases we can indicate Hebrew forms impossible or unattested in Aramaic:

2.1.4.

Verse 3:8 contains a phrase *рѣкохъ къ срьдцу моему*, lit. "I said to my heart," meaning "say to myself" ("And I said to myself, 'If it is thus, how then can my father's god, Mar-Umath, having a head of one stone and [the rest] being made of another stone, save a man, or hear a man's prayer and reward him?'"). It is an obvious Hebraism: *) ואומר אל לבי "and I said to myself," cf. ויאמר ה' אל לבו, lit. "And the Lord said to his heart" (Gen 8:21), לדבר אל לבי "to speak to my heart" (Gen 24:45), ויאמר דוד אל לבו, "and David said to his heart" (1 Sam 27:1), etc. Unlike לאמור בלב "to say in s.-o.'s heart," Gk εἰπεῖν ἐν τῇ διανοίᾳ (which is also found in *ApAb*; cf. 1:4: *помышляхъ въ умѣ своемъ*, and 3:1: *и рӄохъ въ срӄци своемъ*), this idiom was reproduced neither in Aramaic Targums, nor in LXX. Thus, this evidence may support the hypothesis of the Hebrew original of *ApAb*.

2.2. May we retrovert the Hebrew original, omitting the Greek stage?

Normally, we reconstruct first the Greek *Vorlage* and then, when possible, its Semitic original. There are, nevertheless, two kinds of cases where Semitic retroversion may be paradoxically more reliable than Greek (i.e., when the original Semitic forms clearly underlying the Slavonic text are more obvious than the Greek mediatory forms, which may vary):

where the Slavonic version faithfully reproduces obvious Semitisms (or misinterpretations of the Semitic original) which were not found in any extant Greek texts (as, e.g., מר אומתא in 1:3,7,9;3:5,8 נכון in 1:3; אמרתי אל לבי in 3:8 or הביא דבר אל in 2:8);

where the Slavonic text contains citations or parallels to the sources which are preserved only in Hebrew or Aramaic.

Here are four examples: Hebrew-Greek transliteration reflected in the Slavonic text but not attested in Greek (2.2.1.), semantic (2.2.2.) and syntactic (2.2.3.) calques integrated into biblical citations/allusions in *ApAb* which conform to the readings of Hebrew Bible or Aramaic Targums rather than to preserved Greek versions, and a phraseological calque of rabbinic Hebrew (2.2.4.).

2.2.1.

On his way to carve an idol, Terah asks Abraham: *принеси ми сѣчива и* (S om. *al.*) *измала из дома*—"Bring me an ax and <?> from the house" (1:8). CS *сѣчиво* which reproduced ἐγχειρίδιον (Heb חרב) in Exod 20:25 (14th cent.; Srezn:3.905) means there, as well as in our verse, the tool used to hew stone. This use of חרב is not typical for the late Hebrew. Gk πέλεκυς (Heb כשיל or גרזן) for *сѣчиво* (Sin Ps 73:6) would go well with πελεκίζω for *сѣчи* in 1:9 (see comm. *ibid.*). Cf. Ep Jer 15 on the idol holding in his hands both ἐγχειρίδιον and πέλεκυς. The word might have been originally a gloss to the unfamiliar *измала*. The forms *измаала/изымала* are used in Slavonic Num 4:9 for Gk λαβίδας, Heb מלקחים (Lunt 1985:59), which is not appropriate in this context. Moshe Taube proposes rabbinic Heb אזמל 'chisel' (see, e.g., Kelim 13,4). In this case *сѣчиво* = πέλεκυς might be inserted as a gloss to the transliteration ιζμαλ(ος) (?) in 𝔊. This kind of doublet of transliteration and translation occurs in LXX and is very typical for Theodotion (Thackeray 1909:1.31–32).[1]

2.2.2.

In 13:2 Abraham says that, having prepared animals for the sacrifice, he *пождахъ дара вечерняго*, lit. "waited for the evening *gift*." RL translate *даръ вечернии* as "evening gift" (comm. *ibid.*: "or 'reward'; Gk *dōron, dōrea*"). In fact, Gk δῶρον here must mean 'offering,' rendering Heb מנחה meaning both 'gift' and 'offering' (HR:359). Cf. 29:18: *мужи праведны... будуть живущие утвержаеми жрьтвами и **даръми** правды и истины* "The righteous men ... will live, being sustained by the just and thruthful sacrifices and *offerings* [lit. 'gifts']." The word combination must reproduce a Greek calque of biblical Heb מנחת (ה)ערב "evening offering [lit. 'gift']." It was usually rendered by θυσία ἑσπερινή in LXX (in Slavonic versions—*жрьтва вечернѣа*). In our text it designates rather the time of day (before sunset, when the evening sacrifice in the Temple was offered) than the offering itself. See this use in Dan 9:21, where Heb מנחת (ה)ערב "evening offering" is obviously not connected to an actual offering: "While I was still speaking in prayer the man Gabriel ... touched me about the time of evening offering (כעת מנחת הערב); the same usage is attested in Ezra 9:4, 5, etc.

2.2.3.

God says to Abraham: *азъ есмь о тебѣ щитя* "I protect you" or "I am your protector" (9:4). As noted by Rub, CS part. *щитя* here must reflect Heb part. מגן "protecting" of Gen 15:1, being based on a more literal tradition of its translation into Greek than that of LXX (participle in place of conjugated form: ὑπερασπίζω). RL assume that *о тебѣ щитя* reproduces Heb מגן עליך rather

---

[1] Lunt reconstructs the form **изъмало* derived from אזמל. This form can exist only if one of two conditions is observed: (1) the nouns *сѣчива* and *измала* are acc. neut. sg. forms in an *akanie* dialect, which is not possible in the northern, perhaps Novgorodian, text of S; or (2) *сѣчива* and *измала* are neutr. pl. Another possibility is that we are dealing here with one more example of a direct object in the gen. used with the verb *приносити*; cf. *принеси прьста твоего* in *Mar* John 20:27 (Vaillant 1948:#120). Cf. also the same use in SU 4:2 (*принесе цѣны*; see comm. *ibid.*). Thus, we can also posit the form **измалъ* < Gk **ιζμαλ(ος) < Heb אזמל.

than מִגֵּן לָךְ of MT. We can add that this combination was rendered by Aram מִגֵּן עֲלָךְ in *Targum Yerushalmi ad loc.*

2.2.4.

God says to the protagonist: *тебе ради направихъ путь земныи* "for your sake I have indicated the way of earth" (10:14). Lunt (RL) convincingly posits rabbinic Heb דרך ארץ "the way the world operates," also "ethics, manners" (lit. "the way of the earth") for *путь земныи*. Biblical Heb דרך עולם (Ps 139:24) or ארח עולם (Job 22:15), lit. "way of the world" = "eternal/old way" (rendered thus by LXX) are less probable but still possible.

2.3. Two-stage retroversion

While some of the Hebraisms are not attested in any extant Greek text (as in the discussion above), most of them may be found in other Greek translations from Hebrew or Aramaic. As well as Greek equivalents, the Semitic ones may be retroverted on phonetic (transliterations), lexical, syntactic and phraseological levels. We have already □iscussed transliterations above (2.1.1–3; 2.2.3.); below we adduce the examples for semantic, syntactic and phraseological calques.

2.3.1. Semantic calques

2.3.1.1. CS отъ *'from' (1:4)*
Gk ἐκ *'from'*
Heb/Aram -מ *here 'than,' also 'from'*

When the statue of Mar-Umath has fallen down, Abraham "was unable to return him to his place all by himself, since *бяше отъ камени велика тяжокъ*." The untranslated part may mean "he was heavy because of a great stone" according to a well attested use of the prep. *отъ* (Gk ἀπό 'because of'; cf. Slov:2.589,8). Another possible interpretation is: "since he was heavy [having been made] out of a great stone," according to the normal use of ἐκ in Greek—'[made] of' (cf., e.g., Matt 27:29; Rev 18:12). This use is attested more rarely for its regular CS counterpart *отъ*; cf. *престолъ отъ огня* "a throne of fire" (18:3), *отъ камени и отъ дрѣва творени*—ἐκ λίθων καὶ ξύλων (*Supr* 49,27; see more examples in Slov:2.588,4). We propose an alternative interpretation which does not conform to the normal use of the preposition *отъ* in Slavonic, but it could be justified if the Greek *Vorlage* contained ἐκ rendering Heb or Aram prep. -מ 'from, of' and 'than': כי היה כבד מאבן גדולה "since he was heavier than a great stone."

2.3.1.2. CS вышение *(21:5) lit. 'highness'*
Gk ὕψωσις *'highness, majesty'*
Heb גאון *here 'overflow,' also 'majesty, pride'*

In heaven Abraham was shown the whole world including *рѣки и вышения* (S *вышняя al.*) *ихъ*—"rivers and their overflows" (21:5). Rare South Slavic *вышение* occurs in *Supr* 280,30 literally rendering Gk ὕψωσις. Gk ὕψωσ(ις) may go back to Heb גאון generally 'majesty, excellency, pride'; cf., e.g., גאון וגבה "majesty and highness"—ὕψως καὶ δύναμις (Job 40:10(5)), and also more appropriate to our context, 'overflow'; cf. גאון הירדן "overflow of the Jordan" (Jer 12:5; 49:19; 50:44; Zech 11:3) or גאון גליך "overflow of your waves" (Job 38:11).

2.3.1.3. CS основати *'establish' (26:1)*
Gk θεμελιόω *'establish'*
Heb יסד *here 'ordain,' 'appoint,' also 'establish'*

Having seen the allegorical depictions of the sins of Israel, Abraham exlaims: *превѣчне крепче то почто еси основалъ быти тако*—"Eternal, Mighty One! Why did you *ordain* [lit. "establish"] it to be so?" (26:1). CS *еси основалъ*, lit. "establish"—Gk θεμελιόω—Heb יסד, lit. 'found, establish' (cf., e.g., Slavonic versions of Josh 6:25 and Isa 44:28 presented in Srezn:2.732). In later books of the Bible this word, however, means also 'ordain,' 'appoint'—more appropriate to our context (Esth 1:8; Ezra 7:9; 1 Chr 9:22). For other linguistic features of late biblical books reflected in *ApAb* see also comm. to 22:2.

2.3.1.4. CS потъщати *'care for' (27:12)*
Gk σπουδάζω *'care for'*
Heb הבהיל *'trouble'*

Having seen the Temple burnt and Israel captured "because of the idol and murder" (27:7; cf. *b.Yoma* 9b; *Ta'anit* 5a-b), the visionary asks: "Eternal Mighty One! Let the evil works of impiety now pass by ..." (*и рѣхъ превѣчне крѣпче да мимоидутъ* (SU + *нынѣ al.*) *злобия* (SU *злобная al.*) *въ нечьстьи дѣла* A (om. A)) The response looks enigmatic in Slavonic: *и рече къ мнѣ паче праведное время сряцѣть* (SU + *я al.*) *преже преподобьимъ* (SU *подобьимъ al.*) *цѣсарь и въ правдѣ сужу имъ* (SU *судящиимъ al.*) *яже преже създахъ обладати отъ нихъ въ нихъ от техъ же изидуть мужи иже потъщать (потщати* SU) *я елико (внелѣже* SU) *възвѣстихъ тебе и видѣ*—"And he said to me, 'Rather the time of justice will come first with the righteousness of kings. And I shall adjudge to them with justice those whom I earlier created in order to rule thence over them. And from those [kings] will come men who will trouble them, as I made known to you and you saw'" (27:10–12.). Both verses are very obscure. The latter speaks, apparently, of the varying generations of righteous kings and their unrighteous descendants (cf. 9:9). The following data should be taken into account for the different possible interpretations of this verse: (1) CS *паче* (translated here as "rather") may be, less probably, a part of the previous sentence: *и рече къ мнѣ паче* "and he said to me more." (2) a form *цѣсарь* may be nom. or acc. sg. as well as gen. pl.: "In [CS *паче* < Gk παρά] the time of justice the King [= Messiah (?); cf. 29:8–9] will meet them first with the righteousness" according to the majority of mss or "the King will meet the time of justice first with the righteousness" according to SU. (3) *яже преже създахъ* may mean also "whom I initially created"; cf. comm. to 9:3 and Eph 1:4: "he has chosen us in him before the foundation of the world." (4) CS *судити,* Gk κρίνω may mean here not only 'judge' but also 'determine,' 'adjudge.' This usage is obvious in 23:12: *почто еси судилъ сему области такои* "why did you adjudge to this such a power." (5) The use of *обладати + въ* meaning "rule over" may reflect a use of Heb שלט/משל + ב- 'rule over'; cf. 31:2: *властвующая въ нихъ* "ruling over them" and 29:2: *держати въ языцехъ и въ сѣмени твоемъ* "rule over the heathens and over your seed" (for other hebraized uses of CS *въ* in *ApAb* see 12:10, 25:2; cf. Rubinstein 1954:132). (6) *отъ нихъ* may render Gk ἐκ τούτων "since then," "after this," or less probably ἀπὸ τούτων "through them," "by means of them": "... those whom I earlier created in order to rule through them [= kings] over them [= whom I earlier created]...." (7) *въ нихъ* might be either a gloss for *отъ нихъ* or the beginning of the next sentence. (8) The Greek equivalents of CS *срящеть*—ἀπαντάω, ὑπαντάω, συναντάω (Srezn:3.818)—are used with dat., while CS *преподобьимъ* (Gk ὁσιότης, Heb יושר, תום; see HR) of mss SU may be not only instr. sg. but also dat. pl.: "the time of justice will meet first the righteousness of kings." Cf. 1 Kgs 9:4, where Gk ὁσιότης and Heb תום relate to David and Solomon.

Finally, CS *потъщати* regularly rendered Gk σπουδάζω (as trans. normally means 'care for'), which in LXX reproduces Heb בהל (also as trans. in *hiph'il*) 'trouble.' See Slavonic Job 23:16 (Srezn:2.1304): *вседержитель же потщалъ мя* (Gk ἐσπούδασέ με, Heb הבהילני); cf. also LXX and MT in Job 22:10 (Gk ἐσπούδασέ σε Heb יבהלך).

The whole verse in Hebrew would look like this:

ויאמר אלי עוד עת הצדק יבוא תחילה עם מלכי הצדק:

ונתתי להם בצדקה את [העם] אשר יצרתי מראשונה למשול מאז בהם:

ומהם יצאו [גם] האישים אשר יבהלום כאשר הודעתיך וראית.

For more possible Hebrew-Greek semantic calques see 6:3; 13:2; 25:4n.

2.3.2. Syntactic biblicisms

2.3.2.1.

In 4:2 Terah praises Abraham: блг͠слвнъ ты аврааме б͠мъ (б͠гъ богомъ B) моимъ зане принесе цѣну (цѣны SU) бъвъ, lit. "Blessed by my god [or: "to my gods"] are you, Abraham, for you gave honor to [or: "brought the price for"] the gods."[2] The sentence begins with a syntactic biblicism, originally Hebrew, but attested also in Greek and Slavonic versions of Bible. The form богомъ, dat. pl., might have been interpreted as instr. sg. "by my god" (see Phil *ad loc.*). However, the reading "blessed are you by my god" in sg. contradicts the context, where it is the plurality of Terah's gods that is consistently emphasized. This consideration, apparently, caused the scribe of ms B to emend the text to "by the god of my gods" (the reading accepted by Rub as primary). This interpretation might be strengthened by the parallels from *ApAb* 8:3 which has the identical б͡га б͠гомъ (missing in ms S) and from Gen 14:19, where "the most high god" is mentioned in a similar formula of blessing: ברוך אברם לאל עליון "blessed is Abraham of the most high God"). Nevertheless, the *lectio difficilior* of most of the mss should be preferred: the use of the dat. in these copies may be justified by the fact that we are dealing here with the well attested biblical Greek calque of Hebrew: εὐλογημένος (or: εὐλογητός) τοῖς θεοῖς μου—ברוך לאלהי; cf. Gen 14:19; 1 Sam 15:13; 23:21; 2 Sam 2:5; Ps 115:15; Ruth 2:20; 3:10. Greek and sometimes also Slavonic versions of these verses contain forms in *dativus auctoris*, e.g., OB Gen 14:19 has: бл͡венъ аврамъ б͠у вышнему (εὐλογημένος Ἀβραμ τῷ Θεῷ ὑψίστῳ). Thus, the 𝔑 almost literally reproduced Gen 14:19: ברוך אתה אברם לאלהי.

2.3.2.2.

Angel Yahoel reproaches Azazel, who tried to seduce Abraham: укоризна тебе Азазилъ яко часть аврамля на небесехъ а твоя на земли яко ту избра и възлюби въ жилище скверны твоея сего ради дасть тя прѣвечный владыка крѣпкый житель на земли (13:7–8). The last clause is not fully clear. Lunt (1985:60) emends the verse assuming dat. ти in place of acc. тя and creating the ghost-word *жытѣль nom. fem. sg. 'dwelling place' in place of житель 'dweller': "the Mighty One has given you a dwelling on earth." His argument: "the peculiar non-animate accusative житель/жителинъ" and "the odd sense of дасть." Actually, animated masculine nouns of -ĭ declension do not occur in the gen.-acc. in early Old Church Slavonic texts (Vaillant 1948:##64,

---

[2] For the analysis of the second clause see 1.5.1.

119). "Dwelling place" is designated in the same verse by жилище. As far as "the odd sense of дастъ" is concerned, it may be explained by presuming here a syntactic biblicism (cf. Rub ad loc.): נתנך ה' אל גיבור תושב/גר על הארץ—"the Eternal Lord, the Mighty One, has made you a dweller on earth." Heb נתן 'give' and biblical Gk δίδωμι frequently mean also 'set,' 'make,' e.g., Deut 28:1: ונתנך ה' אלהך עליון על הארץ. This Hebraism is attested also in LXX and OB for Deut 28:1: καὶ δώσει σε Κύριος ὁ Θεός σου ὑπεράνω ἐπὶ πάντα τὰ ἔθνη τῆς γῆς—и дастъ ти гъ бг твои надъ всѣми странами земля. Cf. the use of дати (נתן) in 13:11: не о всѣхъ праведницѣхъ данъ еси искушати, lit. "you have been given to tempt not to all the righteous."

2.3.2.3.

CS preposition въ (Gk ἐν) in *ApAb* is often used as Semitic -ב. E.g., in the course of eschatological calculations God says: "I set twelve periods for this impious age to rule over the heathens and over your seed (in Slavonic: держати въ языцехъ и въ сѣмени твоемъ)" (29:2). CS держати въ (here "rule over") is usually translated as "hold among …" However, if CS държати is understood here as Gk συνέχω 'hold, keep,' the verse would not be clear. More probable is Gk κρατέω or one of its synonyms (cf. 10:10: держати левуиафановъ "to rule over the Leviathans"; for дръжати reproducing Gk κρατέω see Slov:1.521; Mikl:178; Srezn:1.775–776) rendering Heb שלט or משל + ב- (Gk ἐν, CS въ) 'rule over.' The same biblicism occurs in 27:11: обладати … в нихъ and in 31:2: властьствующая въ нихъ (lit. "rule in/among"). Cf. Gk ἐξουσιάζω + ἐν as "have power over" in the text of LXX for Heb שלט + ב- (Eccl 2:19; 8:8). For other Hebraized uses of CS въ in *ApAb* see 12:10, 31:4 (CS узрѣти въ lit. "see in s.-th."), going back to Heb/Aram ב- ראה/חזי "see s.-th." (cf. Rubinstein 1954:132); see also 2.3.2.4.

2.3.2.4.

In one of his heavenly visions Abraham saw требник прямо ему и отроци закалаеми на нем въ лице идолу—"an altar opposite it [the idol] and youths slaughtered on it before the idol" (25:2). CS въ лице идолу (translated here "before the idol") literally means "in the face of the idol." CS въ лице is an obvious biblicism: Gk εἰς (τὸ) πρόσωπον, Heb בפני 'before' (cf. MT and LXX Deut 25:9; Hos 5:5; 7:10, etc.). More common Heb לפני is also possible: Heb prep. -ל is rendered by CS въ in 7:8 (see comm. *ibid.*). Cf. the calques of Heb לפני 'before' in *ApAb*: предъ лицемъ (22:2), лицю (23:3).

2.3.3. Phraseological biblicisms

2.3.3.1. *CS* принести куплю *(2:8)*
Gk παρέχειν πρᾶγμα τινί *"to cause trouble to s.-o."*
or
Gk ? < *Heb* הביא דבר אל *"let s.-o. know about the matter"*

This is an example where Greek and Hebrew retroversions both have appropriate (although different) meanings, and it is difficult to make a final decision which one of them to prefer. In ch. 2 Abraham put his fathers idols on his ass; the ass took fright and he ran and threw down the gods (2:2–7). Abraham says: "I have been distressed in my heart, [wondering] *како принесу куплю отцю моему*," lit. "How would I bring the *purchase* to my father?" The sentence is not perfectly clear: *купля* is known to render Greek words for 'purchase,' 'goods,' 'affair,' 'deal,' and 'trade' not fully appropriate to the context. Considering that CS *купля* might have rendered Gk πρᾶγμα (cf. Srezn 1.1371: CS *куплю дѣяти* for Gk πραγματεύσεσθαι in *Pand. Ant.* or CS *безъ купля* for Gk ἀπραγμάτευτος), which regularly reproduced Heb דבר in LXX, *принести куплю* might be a reflection either of the Greek idiom παρέχειν πρᾶγμα τινί "to cause trouble to s.-o." (LSJ:1457) or of the Hebrew idiom הביא דבר אל in the meaning "let s.-o. know about the matter" (Exod 18:19,22,26; *Lev. Rab.* 32), both going well with the context. Thus, two possible translations are: (1) I have been distressed in my heart, [wondering] how would I cause trouble to my father?" (according to the Greek reconstruction); or (2) I have been distressed in my heart, [wondering] how would I let my father know about the matter?" (according to the Hebrew reconstruction).

2.3.3.2. *CS* в горести... душа своея *(6:1)*
Heb במר נפשי *"in the bitterness of my soul"*
cf.
CS горести душа ихъ *(29:15)*
Heb מרת נפשם *"bitterness of their soul"*

There is a biblical idiom which occurs twice, both in aggadic and apocalyptic parts of *ApAb*: *и постенахъ в горести и* (om. S) *в гневе душа своея*—"And I groaned in the bitterness <and> anger of my soul" (6:1.); cf. *стенаниемь горести душа ихъ* "through groaning of the bitterness of their soul" (29:15). For the closest parallels to 6:1 see MT Job 7:11: אשיחה במר נפשי "I shall speak in the bitterness of my soul" (while LXX has ἀνοίξω πικρίαν (or ἐν πικρίᾳ, according to some mss of Lucianic rescension) ψυχῆς μου συνεχόμενος) and Job 10:1: אדברה במר נפשי (LXX: λαλήσω πικρίᾳ ψυχῆς μου συνεχόμενος); cf. also על־מר נפשי in Isa 38:15, במר נפשי in Ezek 27:31 and מרת

נפשו in Prov 14:10 (*Vorlage* of LXX here had apparently מרה נפשו—λυπηρά ψυχὴ αὐτοῦ).

2.3.3.3. CS вергу умъ свои *(6:4)*
Gk ῥίψω τὴν ψυχήν μου
Heb אשלך נפשי *"I shall risk my life"*

Being indignant at his father's idolatry, Abraham says: "Must one put up with evil?[3] Let me risk my life for purity[4] and I shall put forth my own clear thinking before him." (6:4). CS *да вергу умъ свои на чистоту* (lit. "let me throw my mind on the purity") was always translated according to the literal meaning of the Slavonic text. Reconstruction totally changes its sense:

CS *вергу* < Gk ῥίπτω < Heb השליך
CS *умъ* < Gk διάνοια/ψυχή < Heb נפש

The Hebew idiom השליך נפש lit. "throw the soul/oneself," meaning "risk one's life," was literally reproduced by LXX in Judg 9:17: וישלך את נפשו—καὶ ἔρριψεν τὴν ψυχὴν αὐτοῦ . Though נפש is rendered here as ψυχή, it might be translated by διάνοια with the same probability. CS *умъ* regularly renders both words (Srezn:3.1211). Cf. also rabbinic שם נפש 'dedicate oneself.'

2.3.3.4. CS взоръ лица его *(6:15)*
Gk ὁ ὄψις τοῦ προσώπου αὐτοῦ
Heb דמות פניו *(or Aram* צלם אנפוהי *or* זיו אפיו/איקונין) *"his appearance"*

Chapter 6 contains a poetic description of the transformation of a live tree into the senseless idol (a well attested biblical motif, cf., e.g., Isa 44:14–20):
Bar-Eshath, your god, before he was made had been rooted in the ground.

---

[3] CS *единою подобаетъ пострадати зло*. The phrase is obscure. We translated it as if *единою* came in place of *еда*. CS *пострадати зло* was usually translated as "endure evil." This understanding can be supported by the existence of the forms *зълопострадати, злострадати* (Gk κακοπαθεῖν, Slov:1.687; Mikl:229; SRJa11–17:6.32). The form *зло/зъло* was commonly used in place of *зѣло* (Gk μάλα, πολύ, πολλῷ , σφόδρα; see Srezn:1.1000). The alternative reading, thus, may be: "Once it is necessary to suffer heavily."

[4] CS *чистота* (Gk καθαρισμός or ἁγνεία, Heb טהרה) 'purity' must be opposed here to the impurity of idols, the idea found in the Bible and developed in rabbinic writings; cf., e.g., Gen 35:2; *Shabbat* 9,1. On the concept of ritual purity/impurity in *ApAb* see 9:5 ("pure sacrifice"); 13:3, 4 ("impure bird"); 13:8 (earth as a "the dwelling place of your [Azazel's] impurity").

Being great and wondrous, with branches,[5] flowers, and [various] beauties.[6]
And you cut him with an ax, and by your skill the god was made.
And behold, he has dried up, and his sap is gone.
He fell from the heights to the ground, and he went from greatness to insignificance,
and *his appearance* has faded (6:10–15).

---

[5] "With branches"—CS *съвѣемъ* (also *свѣнемъ* AK *съвѣнимь* B). According to the majority of mss it may be understood as *съ* + instr. sg. of the collective *вѣие* 'branches,' 'crown' or of *вѣи* 'branch' (the use of the sg. form may be treated here as a biblicism; cf. the metonymical use of sg. עָנָף 'branch' in Ezek 17:8,23, 31:3). The data of the other mss (and among them ms A, the oldest of the mss containing the fragment) may be interpreted in two ways: (1) *съ вѣнемъ* or *съ вѣнимъ* "with a crown [of tree]." Thus, AK contain CS *hapax legomenon* *вѣнь. RL misinterpret it as "bride-price," "dowry," i.e., *вѣно* (instr. sg. of which would be rather *вѣномъ*). A form *вѣнъ would be identical to the hypothetical Proto-Slavic source of *вѣнокъ*, *вѣньць*, *вѣникъ* (Vasmer:1.291–292). Russ *вѣнъ* means "плетеница изъ ботвы, листвы, зелени съ цвѣтами" (Dal':1.331). (2) *съвѣнимъ* formally may also be treated as a part. *pass. praes.* (cf. praes. *сы* in the same close) meaning 'sold' (or with a nuance of potentiality, 'salable'), derived from *вѣнити* (πωλέω) with perf. forming prefix. The verb might have later been altered by scribal conjectures to the more familiar *съвѣнемъ* and *съвѣемъ*. Thus, the whole verse becomes clearer and we are not forced to emend the word *искореневанъ* ("uprooted," Gk ἐξρίζω, previously translated as 'rooted' with the prefix treated as an early scribal error). The CS text of 6:10–12: *варисатъ же бг҃ъ твои и еще сущу ему преже здѣлания искореневанъ на земли великъ сы и дивенъ съвѣемъ* (*свѣнемъ, съвѣнимь*) *и цвѣты и похвала* (*похвалами А*) *осече же и сѣчивомъ и твоею хитростью створенъ есть бг҃ъ.*

Previous interpretation: Alternative interpretation:

Варисатъ же, богъ твои, и еще сущу ему преже здѣлания, {ис}кореневанъ на земли, великъ сы и дивенъ, съ вѣемъ и цвѣты и похвалами. Осече же и сѣчивомъ. И твоею хитростью створенъ есть богъ.

Варисатъ же, богъ твои, и еще сущу ему преже здѣлания, искореневанъ на земли. Великъ сы и дивенъ съвѣнимъ. И цвѣты и похвала(?) осече же. И сѣчивомъ и твоею хитростью створенъ есть богъ.

"But Bar-Eshath, your god, before he was made, had been rooted in the ground, being great and wondrous, with branches and flowers and <?>. And you cut him with an ax. And by your skill the god was made."

"But Bar-Eshath, your god, before he was made, he had been [lying] uprooted on the ground. Being great and wondrous he was sold. And you cut the flowers and beauties(?). And the god was made with an ax and by your skill.

[6] CS *похвалами*, lit. 'praises,' 'glories.' 'Beauty' may be more appropriate: CS *хвала* 'praise, glory' is attested rendering Gk χάρις (*Ostr* Luke 6:32; John 11:41) which may mean also 'beauty.' There might have been also a mistranslation of acc. χάριν "for sake of" or τούτου χάριν "for this reason": "... it was great and wondrous ... *for this reason* you cut it ..." (cf., e.g., Gal 3:19).

CS *взоръ лица его*, lit. "appearance of his face," we translate as "his appearance." Cf. Heb דמות פניו (*3 En* 35:3 *et pass.*). Similar word combinations are attested in Aramaic texts (and their Greek translations): Gk ὁ ὄψις τοῦ προσώπου αὐτοῦ, Aram צלם אנפוהי (Dan 3:19), ἡ πρόσοψις τῆς εἰκόνος (Th Dan 2:31), ἡ πρόσοψις τοῦ προσώπου (2 Macc 6:18). Gk ὅρασις, μορφή, ὄψις, πρόσοψις render Aram זיו (see LXX and Th Dan 2:31; 3:19; 4:33; 5:6, 9, 10; 7:28). Hence, Aram זיו אפיו (see *j.Yebamot* 15c; *Mo'ed Qatan* 82b; Targum Neophyti Gen 4:5,6; Deut 4:7 and other Palestinian Targums; see Sokoloff 1990:175) or זיו איקונין 'appearance' (*Gen. Rab.* 53; *Exod. Rab.* 35; *Cant. Rab.* to 3:11) are also probable.

2.3.3.5. CS ни силы остави *(6:19)*
καὶ οὐκ ἐκράτησα ἰσχύος
Heb ולא נשאר בו כח or ולא עצר כח *"he retained no strength"*

On the same Bar-Eshath (see previous example), the text continues: *ни силы остави погыбыи собѣ на пагубу* (*погыбе на пагубу* SU)—"he retained no strength utterly perishing" (6:19). For CS *ни силы остави* see LXX and MT of Dan 10:8: Gk καὶ οὐχ ὑπελείφθη ἐν ἐμοὶ ἰσχὺς and καὶ οὐκ ἐκράτησα ἰσχύος—Heb ולא נשאר כח and לא עצרתי כח. CS *на пагубу*; cf. Heb עדי אבד (Num 24:20, 24). The ת might look as follows: ולא עצר כח אבד עדי אבד.

2.3.3.6. CS того въ бг҃ положу *(7:9)*
Heb אשימנו לאלהים *"I shall make him into god"*

Reflecting on the hierarchy of luminaries, Abraham declares: "I would not make it [sun] into a god either [*ни того въ бг҃ положу* (SUD *того бм҃ъ нареку al.*)], since its course is obscured [both] at night [and] by the clouds" (7:9). There is a Hebraism in the oldest copy, lit. "I shall put it into a god"—Heb אשימנו לאלהים. Cf. the same construction (Heb שם + ל- "make s.-o. into s.-th.") in Gen 21:13, 18; 45:8, 9; Exod 2:14; Deut 10:22; Judg 11:11; Isa 41:15; 60:15; Jer 25:9; Ps 18:44, etc. The LXX normaly has ποιέω "make" in place of Heb שם "put" (cf. ποιέω + εἰς for Heb שם ל- rendered by *сътворити* + *въ* in OB Gen 21:13, 18; 46:3), although sometimes it renders Heb שם literally: by καθίστημι or τίθημι (cf., e.g., in "*d*-Gruppe" of the Göttingen edition in Gen 21:18 or in most mss of Exod 2:11 and Judg 11:11). Heb ל- is rendered by *въ* also in *ApAb* 7:9. Cf. a similar syntactic calque in 20:5: *положю сѣмени твоему языкъ людии* (see next paragraph 2.3.3.7.).

2.3.3.7 *CS* положю сѣмени твоему языкъ людии *(20:5)*
 Heb ושמתי לזרעך את קהל עמים *"and I shall make the company of nations to be your seed"*

God promises Abraham: *положю сѣмени твоему языкъ* (SU *языки al.*) *людии* (SU om. *al.*)—"I shall make your seed into a company of nations" (29:5).[7] There is the same Hebraism as in 7:9 (שם + ל- "make s.-o. into s.-th."): *того въ бг положу* "I shall make it into a god" (Heb אשימנו אלהים), although in 7:9 Heb ל- is rendered by *въ* and here by dat. (cf. 7:8; 22:2; 23:3; 25:2). Cf. לגוי (Gen 32:13); ושמתי את-זרעך כחול הים (Gen 13:16); ושמתי את-זרעך כעפר הארץ גדול אשימך (Gen 46:3). Thus, the Hebrew text might have a paraphrase of these verses: ושמתי את זרעך לקהל עמים, according to which it was translated above. If we assume, however, that the Slavonic text preserves here the grammatical structure of the original, the original would look like this: ושמתי לזרעך את קהל עמים "And I shall turn the company of nations to be your seed," which may reflect quite a different historiosophic conception.

2.3.3.8. *CS* и годѣ бысть лицю моему
 lit. *"and it was pleasing to my face" (23:3)*
 Heb וייטב לפני *"and it was pleasing to me"*

God says on the creation (or idea of creation): "it was pleasing to Me"—*и годѣ бысть предъ лицемъ моимъ*, lit. "and it was pleasing before my face" (22:2). Cf. 23:3: *яко то годѣ бысть лицю моему*, lit. "what was pleasing to my face." 𝔐 in both cases must have וייטב לפני, lit. "be good/pleasing to the face of [= before] s.-o." Heb ל- is rendered by a preposition in 22:2 and by dat. in 23:3 (cf. 7:8; 20:5; 25:2). CS *годѣ* (*гви*) reproduced Gk ἀρεστόν (κυρίῳ), Heb (ה') ייטב בעיני in Lev 10:19, ms 14th cent. (Srezn:1.540) or Gk ἀρέσκω, Heb טוב בעיני- in Gen 19:8, ms 14th cent. (Srezn:1.540). Cf. also Gk ἀρεστός 'pleasing,' ἀρκέω 'be pleasing,' and Heb -ייטב/טוב/ישר בעיני lit. "(be) good in the eyes of s.-o." in Gen 16:6; Deut 6:18; Exod 15:26, etc. Heb יטב לפני- is found only in late biblical Hebrew (Esth 5:14; Neh 2:5,6).

2.3.3.9. *CS* въ чисмени lit. *"in number" (29:17)*
 Gk ἐν ἀριθμῷ
 Heb במספר *"by [exact] count" or "in [prescribed] number"*

According to 29:17, in the eschatological future the righteous men will be kept by God "by number"—*въ чисмени*, lit. "in number." Heb במספר, rendered

---

[7] On "company of nations" see comm. to 29:5.

in LXX by ἐν ἀριθμῷ, may mean "by [exact] count" (Deut 25:2; 2 Sam 2:15; Isa 40:26; 1 Chr 9:28) or "in [prescribed] number" (Num 29:18; Ezra 3:4). Cf. the same calque in *OB* Deut 25:2: *въ число*.

See also phraseological biblicisms in 8:3 (CS *въ умѣ срдца своего*—Gk ἐν τῇ σοφίᾳ / διανοίᾳ καρδίας σοῦ—Heb בחכמת לבך) and 17:18 (CS *сияти свѣтъ*—Gk φαίνω φῶς—Heb האיר אור "make light to shine") analysed in other chapters.

Chapter 3
Textual Criticism and Retroversion

Very often the dependence between the arguments of textual criticism and retroversion is bilateral. Here we adduce the examples where textual choices are made on the basis of retroversions.

3.1.

When the idol Bar-Eshath appointed to keep the fire, eventually fell to it, Abraham mocked him: and "while I [Abraham] was speaking laughingly, he [idol Bar-Eshath] was *gradually* [*помалу* (+ *помалу* B)] burned up by the fire and became ashes" (5:11). The reading of ms B is not a dittography but a syntactic calque going back to the Hebrew original; cf. LXX Deut 7:22: κατὰ μικρὸν μικρόν; MT: מעט מעט 'little by little,' 'gradually' (*OB* has *помалу домала*).

3.2.

Abraham tells Terah: "I shall seek in your presence the God [*възищу* (SUD *възвѣщу al.*) *предъ тобою бога*] who created all gods" (7:11). Ms S contains a biblicism which was not understood in most of the mss (which have *възвѣщу* 'claim'): אדרש את/אל/ל/ב אל(הים) (MT, *pass.*); cf., e.g., Job 5:8: אולם אני אדרש אל אל ולאלהים אשים דברתי "I shall seek God and to God will I put my speech" (while LXX has δεηθήσομαι Κυρίου). Cf. *творца ты ищеши* (8:3), *изискати мене* (9:6).

God praises Abraham: "*бга бгомъ* (*бо* SI) *и* (om. ACIU) *творца ты* (om. KO) *ищеши въ умѣ срдца своего* (SUD *въ уме своемъ* AC)—"In the wisdom of your heart you are searching for the God of gods and the Creator" (8:3). The obscure in Slavonic *въ умѣ срдца своего* of mss SUD must go back to Gk ἐν τῇ διανοίᾳ (or σοφίᾳ) καρδίας σου and Heb בחכמת לבך (or Aram / בחכימות ליבך דליבך בחכימא); cf. חכמת לב in Exod 35:35. Thus, the ℵ might have contained: את אלהי האלהים ואת הבורא בחכמת לבך דרשת. For the idea that Abraham had been "searching for God" in "the wisdom of his heart" even before God addressed him in Gen 12:1 see *Jub* 12; Philo, *De Abr.* 69–70; Josephus, *Ant.* 1,154–157; *Gen. Rab.* 39:1.

3.3.

Here is a passage from the "Song of Abraham" (17:8–21), recited by angel Yahoel and Abraham, when they had arrived in heaven: тъ (S ты *al.*) свѣтъ сияеши предъ утрьнимъ (SU внутренимъ *al.*) свѣтомъ на тварь свою (+ и A) от лица твоего дневати¹ на земли (от … земли om. S) а на небесныхъ жилищихъ твоихъ (om. S) бескуденъ етеръ свѣтъ отъ (om. SAKO) зарьства неисповѣдима отъ свѣтовъ лица твоего—"You make the light shine before the morning light upon your creation <from your face in order to bring the day on the earth>. And in <your> heavenly dwellings there is an inexhaustible other light of an inexpressible splendor from the lights of your face" (17:18–19). CS тъ (S ты *al.*) свѣтъ сияеши sometimes is translated as "You, O Light, shine" (Bonw; BL; Phil). We prefer the reading of ms S for the following reasons: (1) CS сияти may function as a causative verb rendering Gk φαίνω (see Mikl:842; Srezn:3.362); (2) CS сияти свѣтъ may reproduce Gk φαίνω φῶς and Heb האיר אור, both well attested (cf., e.g., MT and LXX in Ezek 32:7).

The following CS предъ утрьнимъ (SU внутренимъ *al.*) свѣтомъ according to most of the mss has to be translated "before the *inner* light." "Inner light," although attested in *Jos. Asen.* 6:6, has there a meaning implausible in our context. "Before the *morning* light" of ms S has more intertextual corroboration: Heb עד אור הבוקר (Gk ἕως φωτὸς τοῦ πρωΐ) is a common biblical idiom (1 Sam 25:34,36; 2 Sam 17:22; 2 Kgs 7:9). The verse must refer to the midrashic motif of the "special light of creation," by which God illuminated all that he created even before the luminaries had been made; see Aristobulus, *Fragment* 3; *4 Ezra* 6:40; Josephus, *Ant.* 1:27,2; *3 En*(J)25:3; *b.Hagigah* 12a, etc. Cf. also one of the interpretations of 9:3.

The contradiction arising from the fact that the "light" first mentioned and the "other light" both emanate from God's face could be solved by the assumption that "from your face" in 17:18 is a pronominal Heb מלפניך "from you" (Rub *ad loc.*). The whole phrase in Hebrew would look like this:
המאיר אור עד אור הבוקר על יצירך מלפניך להביא יום על פני הארץ:
ובמשכנות מרומיך שפעת אור אחר מזיו נגהות פניך

---

¹ The ambiguous use of the infinitive дневати (CS *hapax legomenon* translated here as "[in order] to bring the day") may be explained by *infinitivus finalis* in Hebrew. Cf. Gen 1:15: להאיר על הארץ "… in order to bring light upon the earth." The infinitive of purpose used alone (i.e., without ἵνα, ὡς, etc.) is attested also in Jewish Gk texts; cf. Moulton *et al.*:3.134–135.

3.4.

In 20:5 God promises Abraham: *положю сѣмени твоему языкъ* (SU *языки al.*) *людии* (SU om. *al.*)—"I shall make your seed[2] into a company of nations" (29:5). Mss SU have *языкъ людии*, lit. "a nation of peoples." BL state: "S adds (after *nation*) *of people* wrongly." *Lectio difficilior* of SU, however, may reflect something like Heb לשון גוים; cf. Zech 8:23: לשונות גוים (αἱ γλῶσσαι τῶν ἐθνῶν) or קהל עמים and קהל גוים, used in a context similar to that of *ApAb* in Gen 28:3; 35:11; 48:4 (συναγωγή ἐθνῶν) or in Ezek 23:24 (ὄχλος λαῶν) and Jer 50:9. Heb עדת לאומים (Ps 7:8) or המון לאומים (Ps 65:8) are also possible. "The seed of Abraham" is defined as lit. "the nation(s) of peoples" (*языкомъ ... людии*) also according to our interpretation of 24:1. Rub brings the analogous Lat *populus nationum* from the Vulgate for Gen 35:11 (קהל גוים).

See also 1:1; 1:3; 2:3; 6:7; 7:9; 10:2, 3; 20:5; 27:3; 28:5.

---

[2] See note to 20:5.

Chapter 4
Intertextual Verification as a Tool of Retroversion

One of the most important tools of retroversion is intertextual verification on the level of original. Most of the retroversions brought above are confirmed to a greater or lesser extent by the parallels either contemporary to the original or belonging to the tradition common with the original. Here we present the examples where the intertextual analysis has a decisive significance.

4.1. Biblical paraphrases

4.1.1.

In his speech rejecting idolatry, Abraham exclaims: *что си лихоть дѣяния еже дѣеть отьць мои* (3:2). The verse is not clear in Slavonic. To avoid interpreting the problematic *лихоть*, Tikhonravov proposed nom. *дѣяние* in place of gen. *дѣяния* and reads *лихоть* as *ли хоть*: *что си ли хоть дѣяние еже дѣеть отьць мои* "what is the deed which my father is doing?" The words with the root **lix-* in Slavic languages lie in the semantic areas of either 'excessiveness, superfluity' or 'evil' (Vasmer:3.505). In the late ms K *лихоть дѣяния* is interpreted according to the second possibility, as *злодеяние* 'evil deed,' and most of the modern translators follow this interpretation. As for *лихоть* per se, Srezn mentions only one source with its Greek counterpart ἀνομαλία (*Zlatostruj* 12th cent.; Srezn:s.v.), while the adverbial combination *въ лихоть* rendering Gk περιττῶς/περισσῶς 'superfluously' is much better attested. Cf. also *лихъ* περισσός, *лихо* περισσόν, *лихнути* περισεύω, *лихотъкъ* ὑπερβολή, and *лихва* τόκος (Slov:2.124–128; Mikl:338–339). Therefore, *лихоть* might very well reproduce Gk περίσσεια, regularly used to translate Heb יתרון or בצע 'profit' in LXX (for sources in abundance see HR:s.v.). Thus, the verse almost verbatim cites Eccl 1:3. MT: מה יתרון לאדם בכל עמלו שיעמל (LXX: τίς περίσσεια τῷ ἀνθρώπῳ ἐν παντὶ μόχθῳ αὐτοῦ ᾧ μοχθεῖ; *OB*: *что изобилие чл͠ку въ всемъ трудѣ его еже трудится*) "what is the profit for a man in all his labor which he is doing?" Thus, the Greek *Vorlage* and the Hebrew original would look like this:

𝔊: τίς περίσσεια ἐν τῷ μόχθῳ ᾧ μοχθεῖ πατήρ μου
ℌ: מה יתרון בעמלו שיעמל אבי
"What is the profit of the labor which my father is doing?"

4.1.2.

"And he [Terah] made five other gods, and he gave them to me [Abraham] and told me to sell them outside in the street of the town [*внѣ на пути градьсцѣмъ* (S *градьстѣмъ al.*)]. And I ... went out to the main road to sell them" (2:1–2). CS *путь градьскыи* rendering Gk ἡ ὁδὸς τῆς πόλεως must be translated here not as "the town road" or "the way to the town" (like דרך (ה)עיר of Ezek 21:24(19) or 1 Kgs 8:44=2 Chr 6:34) but rather as "the street of the town," according to one of the meanings of ὁδός which is attested more frequently in late Greek and which is the primary meaning of the word in Modern Greek. Cf. CS *на пути градьсцѣмъ* and Heb ברחובה של העיר "on the street of the town" of *Ta'anit* 2,1. Thus, we get rid of the contradiction between the elements of the double designation of the destination, since CS *внѣ* (Gk ἔξω, ἔξωθεν, ἐξωτέρω) must go back to Heb בחוץ (cf. Prov 7:12; Isa 51:23; Jer 11:16), which refers to the area *inside* the town. The doublet of בחוץ and ברחוב is very frequent in MT and usually rendered in LXX by ὁδός and πλατεῖα: בחוץ בתוך רחבות "outside in the streets" (Prov 22:13), פעם בחוץ פעם ברחבות "once outside and once in the street" (Prov 7:12), ובכל חוצות...בכל רחבות "in all streets and everywhere outside" (Amos 5:16), בחוצות...ברחובות "outside and in the streets" (Nah 2:5), etc.; cf. also בשוקים וברחובות (Cant 3:2). Based on these parallels we can retrovert the text:

𝔊: ἔξω ἐν τῇ ὁδῷ τῆς πόλεως
ℌ: בחוץ ברחובה של העיר
"outside in the street of the town"

Thus, *путь градскыи* "street of the town" of 2:1 is opposed to *гостинець* 'main road, highway' of 2:2: Abraham does not follow his father's order and, despite it, sells the gods on the road outside the town.

4.1.3.

When Abraham first heard the voice of God talking to him, he said: *и уже сужасе ся* (*уже се* S *се уже* U) *дхъ мои и избѣже дша моя отъ мене*—"my spirit was affrighted, and my soul fled from me" (10:2). *Lectio difficilior* in SU might reproduce *ужже* (*ужьже*) *си* 'burnt' of the prototext modified in other mss by a scribal conjecture to *ужасе ся* 'affrighted.' Cf. the same form in 8:6 (*и ужьже*). Other mss contain *ужасе ся* 'affrighted': "and my soul was very affrighted." The last reading can be confirmed by Ps 6:4: "and my soul was affrighted"—καὶ ἡ ψυχή μου ἐταράχθη—as ונפשי נבהלה. The second clause (*и избѣже дша моя отъ мене*) can be also corroborated intertextually: cf. Cant 5:6: "my soul went out [from me]"—ψυχή μου ἐξῆλθεν—יצאה נפשי (*OB: дша моя изыиде*). 𝔐: נבהלה רוחי ונפשי יצאה ממני.[1]

See also comm. to 2:8; 6:4; 8:3; 9:3; 17:18; 20:4.

4.2. Parallels from Pseudepigrapha

Verses 11:2–3 contain a detailed description of the chief angel Yahoel guiding Abraham: "The appearance of his body was like sapphire, and the likeness of his face like chrysolite, and the hair of his head like snow, and a turban on his head like the appearance of the bow in the clouds, and the closing of his garments [like] purple, and a golden staff [was] in his right hand"—*и бяше видѣние тѣла ногу* (om. BSU) *его аки* (AC om. *al.*) *санфиръ и взоръ лица его яко хрусолитъ и власи главы его яко снегъ и кидаръ на голове его яко видѣние лука облачна и одѣяние ризъ его багоръ и жезлъ златъ въ десници его*. In most mss the verse begins with the words: *бяше видѣние тѣла ногу его аки* (AC om. *al.*) *санфиръ*. Previously the obscure *ногу* (which might have been understood as gen. dual. 'feet') here was ignored (as it was ignored by the scribes of B and S) and the phrase was translated as "the appearance of his body was like sapphire." However, *lectio difficilior* of mss ACDIHK—*видение тѣла ногу его*—does make sense in Slavonic, where it might go back to *scriptio continua*: *видение тѣла ногуева* "the appearance of the griffin's body." CS *ногъ* or *ногуи* is attested reproducing Gk γρύψ (in LXX Lev 11:13 and Deut 14:12 the Greek word stands for Heb פרס—a kind of bird of prey).

Angels looking like eagles are mentioned in Ezek 1:10; *3 En* 2:1; 24:11. This reading, nevertheless, supposedly contradicts the following description, where the bird-like angel has "hair on his head" (*власи главы его*) and hands (*и жезлъ златъ въ десници его*); cf. also 10:4: "the angel he sent to me in the likeness of a man." Thus, this reading could not be understood by the scribes, who were not acquainted with the tradition of Jewish angelology: only the torso of Yahoel must be of griffin-like appearance, while his head is like that of a man; cf. *3 En* 26:3, where the angel Serapiel, prince of the Seraphim, is described as follows: "his face is like the face of angels, and his body is like the body of eagles (Heb נשרים)" (the rest of the description is also very similar to that of the angel Yahoel here); cf. *3 En* 47:4: "their faces were like angels' faces, and their wings like birds wings." Cf. also the combined human-eagle nature of the souls in *3 En* 44:3: "their faces looked like human faces, but their bodies were like eagles."

---

[1] On the use of *душа* "soul" and *духъ* "spirit" in *ApAb* see comm. to 6:3.

See also comm. to 15:7; 17:18; 27:3.

4.3. Parallels from Jewish Hellenistic sources

4.3.1.

In heaven Abraham was shown allegoric images belonging to the main points of human history; in 23:5–8 he "saw there a man very great in height and terrible in breadth, incomparable in aspect, entwined with a woman who was also equal to the man in aspect and size. And they were standing under a tree of Eden, and the fruit of the tree was like the appearance of a bunch of grapes of vine. And behind the tree was standing, as it were, a serpent in form, but having hands and feet like a man, and wings on its shoulders: six on the right side and six on the left. And he was holding in his hands the grapes of the tree and feeding the two whom I saw entwined with each other." Abraham asks Yahoel for explanation, and he gives his answer: *се есть свѣтъ чл͠вчь (сл͠нце B) се есть адамъ и се есть помышьление ихъ на земли си есть евьга* (23:10). The verse was misinterpreted before: key definitions *свѣтъ чл͠вчь* and *помышьление ихъ на земли* were translated previously as "the human world" and "their desire upon the earth" (BL), "penchant [Gk διαβούλιον —Heb יצר] des hommes" and "leur convoitise sur terre" (Phil), "la lumière, le soleil [according to ms B]" and "l'objet de leur desire sur la terre" (Rub), "the world of men" and "their thought on earth" (RL). Actually, CS *с(ъ)вѣтъ* here as well as in 22:2; 23:14; 26:5; 29:10 most probably renders Gk βουλή (Slov:4.243–244; Mikl:916; Srezn:3.681), Heb עצה, דעת, מחשבה (HR:227–228), while CS *помышьление* means here rather 'desire' than 'thought.' This word rendered either Gk ἐπιθυμία (cf. *Supr* 296,1 and Slavonic versions of Matt 5:28; Lam 1:7—Heb מחמד; Dan 9:23—Heb חמודה) or διάνοια (Heb יצר, in Gen 8:21: *помышление чл͠цско—*ἡ διάνοια τοῦ ἀνθρώπου—יצר לב האדם "the desire of the man's heart"; see Srezn:2.1171). The most common equivalents for Gk ἐπιθυμία in MT are Heb תאוה, חשק, רצון (HR:521), while Gk διάνοια renders Heb יצר (1 Chr 29:18). Thus, *ApAb* might refer here to an allegorical conception very similar to the idea of Philo of Alexandria, according to which Adam and Eve symbolize correspondingly "reason" (νοῦς) and "passion" (αἴσθησις); see Philo, *Leg. All.* II,10,14; *Quis Her.* 11. The dichotomy of "reason" (λογισμός) and "passion" (πάθος) is found also in 4 Macc 2.

4.3.2.

One more parallel to Philo probably occurs in 6:3. Abraham wonders why his father Terah persists in worshiping idols: *или убо тѣло повинулъ будеть своеи дши и дшю дхови а дха безумью и* (om. S) *невѣжествию*—"would he have subordinated his body to his soul, his soul to his spirit, then his spirit—to folly and ignorance?" CS *духъ* 'spirit' and *душа* 'soul' go back to ψυχή and πνεῦμα in the Greek *Vorlage* and to רוח and נשמה (or נפש) in the hypothetical Hebrew original. H̄, therefore, might have: שעבד את נפשו לרוחו ורוח להוללות ושכלות. This description is reminiscent of Philo's (originally Platonic; cf. Rub *ad loc.*) views on the tripartite hierarchical nature of the soul which consists of the highest, rational, part—νοῦς—and two spiritual parts of different grades (πνοή and πνεῦμα); see *Leg. Al.* I, 12–13 *et pass.*[2]

Wohlberg (1902:32) posits that the trichotomy of the non-physical part of man expressed in the hierarchy of נפש— נשמה—רוח might be common to both the Bible and rabbinic thought. Similar ideas were also developed in medieval Jewish thought (cf., e.g., Sa'adia Gaon, *Emunot ve-De'ot*, 6). Thus, here הוללות ושכלות "folly and ignorance" (Eccl 1:17) must stand in place of νοῦς; otherwise we are dealing here with a diarchic soul structure, also well attested; see Wis 15:11; 1 Thes 5:23; Heb 4:12; *b. Haggiga* 12a, *Nidda* 31a; *3 En* passim (see Odeberg 1928:174–180); cf. also *ApAb* 10:2. (Cf. the following section.)

4.4. Parallels from Rabbinic sources

4.4.1.

At the very beginning of the writing Abraham is depicted as an idol-worshiper:[3] *въ время прилучения жребия моего егда скончевахъ службы требы оца моего фары бмъ его древянымъ и каменымъ златымъ и сребренымъ мѣдянымъ и железнымъ въшедъ въ црквь ихъ на службу* ... "at the time when my lot came up, when I had finished the services of my father Terah's sacrifice to his gods of wood, stone, gold, silver, brass, and iron, having entered their temple for the service ..." (1:2–3). CS combination *службы требы* translated here as "the services of sacrifice," is not fully clear. Tikhonravov contends that *требы* "is surely a gloss," despite the fact that both

---

[2] Another possibility is that Heb נפש (Gk πνεῦμα, ψυχή, CS *душа*) here was just a reflexive form—'himself' (it is attested to be literally rendered in Jewish Gk texts; cf. Moulton *et al.*:3.43). Considering that שעביד נפשיה (reconstructed from CS *повинулъ дшю*) in rabbinic sources means 'bound himself,' 'make himself responsible' (Jastrow 1903:1609) and רוח שטות means 'folly, madness' (*ibid.*:1553) we can reconstruct Heb שעביד נפשו לרוח שטות (or Aram דשטותא שעביד נפשיה לרוח) "he bound himself to folly." Thus, these three concepts—נפש 'soul'/'himself,' רוח 'spirit,' שטות 'folly'—might be brought into hierarchic relationships by later copyists or translators.
[3] Cf. *Jub* 12; *Gen. Rab.* 38:13; *Tanna debe Eliahu* 2:25; *Seder Eliahu Rabba* 33.

words are well known in Slavonic. Bonw believes that *требы* might have replaced *требища* "of the altar." It seems more useful to consider the whole of the word combination to be a calque of something like *) λειτουργίαι θυσίας rendering Heb *) עבודות הקרבן or, less probably, ἐργασία λειτουργίας – מלאכת (ה)עבודה (Exod 35:24; 36:3; 1 Chr 9:13,19). Cf. Heb עבודת הקרבנות "the service of sacrifices" (*Exod. Rab.* 30) and slightly different Gk θυσίᾳ καὶ λειτουργίᾳ (Phil 2:17). The change of grammatical conjunction by derivation (and vice versa) in Slavonic translations is well attested; cf., e.g., *съвѣтъмь людьскыимь* < τῇ βουλῇ καὶ τῷ δημοσίῳ (*Efr. korm.* 87,2). Thus, the whole verse becomes clearer: having finished the "sacrificial services" outside the temple, Abraham enters the temple to continue the service inside.

This description precisely follows the order of the Second Temple daily morning *tamid* service as it is described in the Mishna: first, priests cast lots (*Yoma* 2, 1–4; *Tamid* 1, 1–2; cf. also Luke 1:9), then they sacrifice in front of the sanctuary (*Tamid* 1–5), finishing their service inside (*Tamid* 6). Cf. the evocation of priestly lots in similar context in later midrash: "After a time, *the lot fell to Terah* to go and serve idols for the wicked Nimrod ..." (Margulies 1947:205). Cf. similar anachronistic "[time] of evening offering" (Heb מנחת (ה)ערב)) in 13:3. For other evocations of the Temple and its service see 25:4; 27:1–5; 29:18.[4]

4.4.2.

Ordering Abraham to fulfill a sacrifice ("Covenant between the Pieces"), God promises him: *тои требѣ положю ти (положи ти D) вѣки[5] и възвѣщю ти съблюденая (съблюдения ACDK)*—"In this sacrifice I shall set before you the ages and make you know *secrets* [?]" (9:6). CS *съблюденая*, lit. 'kept

---

[4] It is less probable that by *сконцевахъ службы требы ѡца моего* "I finished my father Terah's sacrificial services" Abraham means his rejection of idol worshiping. In this case, by *прилучение жребия* the "lot" of the divine choice would be meant (cf. the use of the word "lot" with this meaning in *ApAb* 29:21; Deut 18:2; Dan 12:13; Acts 8:21). This interpretation goes well with the second variant of the interpretation of *настръзающи*— "to destroy" (see comm. to 1:1): thus, the first two verses tell us that it was the day when Abraham destroyed the gods, testing them (cf. 1:6, 2:9, 5:9) and ceased serving them when the lot of heavenly choice had fallen upon him.

[5] Cf. *покажю* (< *положю*?) *ти векы* "I shall show you the ages" (9:9), *вi года положихъ вѣка сего* "I set 12 periods of this age" (28:2). CS *вѣкы* may render here Gk αἰῶνας, Heb עולמים 'ages' or 'worlds.' Cf. 9:9 and apocalyptic descriptions of celestial and lower *worlds* and historical *ages* below. However, the most widespread meaning of CS *вѣкъ* is 'life.' This meaning is the most appropriate for CS *вѣкъ* in 17:17–18 (twice). The plural form in 9:5 might also go back to the *pluralia tantum* of Heb חיים. Thus, the verse might have been the allusion to Deut 30:15: "I set before you today life and good, death and evil."

things,' may go back either to (1) Heb נצורות (Isa 48:6; Aram נטירן in Targums; not reflected in the main versions of LXX) or Aram טמירתא, מטמרן, 'kept,' 'hidden' = 'secret things' of Targums for Heb נסתרות (Deut 29:28) or, less probably, to (2) Heb משפטים 'observances' (according to mss ACDK). Various Greek mediatory translations for both possibilities may be found; see Slov:4.215; Srezn:3.644–645. RL suggest Gk (συν)τηρέμενα, which goes better with the last interpretation. However, the usage of the same word in 23:3—*съблюденая въ срдци моемь* 'kept in my heart'—confirms the first two interpretations.

Cf. in the very similar context in *Hekhalot Rabbati* 16:1: ואומ' לפניהם הרזים הסתורים "and I shall tell them the secrets and mysteries." On the angel Metatron (whose functions are identical to those of Yahoel; see ch. 10) revealing to an apocalyptic seer the secrets of heaven see Odeberg (1928:103); for the secret places of heaven called מסתתריםsee *Lam. Rab.*, intr. 24.; Metatron himself is called מסטורין, מסטירין in *Gen. Rab.* 5,2. The understanding of "Covenant between the Pieces" (Gen 15) as a revelation of divine secrets is found, e.g., in Philo, *Her.*, 258, 266; *4 Ezra* 3:13–15; cf. *Gen. Rab.* 44:12.

4.4.3.

Having seen the allegorical images of human sins and their punishments, Abraham raises his voice against God's justice and says: "Eternal, Mighty One! Why did you ordain it to be so? Take back these testimonies!" (26:1). Then God asks him: "Hear, Abraham, and understand what I tell you, and answer whatever I ask you! Why did your father Terah not listen to your voice and abandon the demonic idolatry until he perished, and all his house with him?" (26:2–3) Abraham answers: "Eternal Mighty One! Evidently because he did not will to listen to me, nor did I follow his deeds." (26:4) And here comes the concluding cue of God, which is the key phrase of the whole chapter: *яко свѣтъ оца твоего въ немь* (+ *бысть* D) *якоже твои свѣтъ в тебѣ тако и моея воля свѣтъ въ мнѣ* (+ *есть* SU) *готовъ бываетъ въ дни приходящая преже и* (om. DCU) *тѣхъ не увеси ни будущихъ в ня* (26:5). The most obscure here are: *моея воля свѣтъ въ мнѣ* (cf. 22:2: *се есть воля моя к сущему во свѣтѣ*; both phrases can hardly be explained on the level of a Semitic original) and *готовъ бываетъ*. CS *с(ъ)вѣтъ*—Gk βουλή we translate here as 'will,' although 'reason,' 'counsel' might be also appropriate. In early Christian Gk βουλή was used as "(free) will," "(evil) impulse," "will (of God)" (Lampe:302). CS *воля* must render Gk θέλημα (Esth 1:8) or θέλησις (cf. Heb רצון in Prov 8:35; 2 Chr 15:15 or חפץ in Ezek 18:23); see Srezn:1.298; SDRJa11–14:1.472–474. The combination of both (*воля*—θέλημα and *свѣтъ*—βουλή) is attested in the very similar context of Eph 1:11: ... προορισθέντες κατὰ πρόθεσιν τοῦ τὰ πάντα ἐνεργοῦντος κατὰ *τὴν βουλὴν τοῦ θελήματος αὐτοῦ* "... predestined according to the purpose of him who does all things according to *the will desired by him*." The idea of our verse becomes fully clear, when the following готовъ бываетъ (previously invariably interpreted as "is ready") is retroverted. It is, obviously, a calque of Gk ἕτοιμόν ἐστιν 'inevitable,' 'sure to come' (on ἕτοιμος + εἰμί or γίγνομαι see LSJ:704; Dvoretskij:1.680). The Slav translator was apparently misled by the use of this idiom in NT, where ἕτοιμόν εἰμι means only "be ready"; cf. Greek and Slavonic versions of Luke 22:33 (*Zogr, Mar, Nik*); Matt 24:44 (*Zogr, Mar, As, Ostr*) and 2Cor 12:14 (*Slepz, Šiš*). The translation of the whole verse will look like this: "As the will of your father is in him, as your will is in you, so also the will desired by me is inevitable in coming days which you will not know in advance, nor the things which are in them." Hence, we are dealing here with the rabbinic conception of free will combined with the inevitability of God's will (predetermination). The idea is most clearly expressed in *Abot* 3:5: הכול צפוי והרשות נתונה "Everything is predestined, but freedom is given."[6]

See also comm. to 10:3; 17:18; 27:3; 29:8.

4.5. Parallels from non-Jewish sources

Reflecting on the hierachy of idols Abraham mentions one named "Zouch" or "Zouche":

For behold, Zoukh [*Зоухе* SU *Зоухъ al.*], my brother Nahor's god, is more honored than your [Terah's] god Mar-Umath, since he is made of gold sold by men. And if he becomes worn out with the years,[7] he will be remade, whereas Mar-Umath,[8] if he is changed or broken, will not be remade, since he is of stone. [And] what about Yoavon,[9] a god <who is in the power of another god>,[10] who stands beside Zoukh [*Зоухеемъ/Зоухиемъ*]? (6:7–9)

---

[6] The same idea is probably reflected also in *Pss. Sol.* 9:4: "Our works are in the choosing and power of our souls, to do right and wrong in the works of our hands, and you in your rightneousness oversee human beings."

[7] *обетшаетъ лѣтомъ*. Lit. "... with the year (sg.)." Cf. Aram עתיק יומין/יומיא, Gk (ὁ) παλαιὸς ἡμερῶν, CS (*GB*) ветхии дньми (Dan 7:9,13,23) and Heb בא בימים, Gk προβεβηκώς ἡμερῶν (Gen 18:11; 24:1; Josh 13:1; 23:1–2; 1 Kgs 1:1). Biblical Heb/Aram ימים/ימין, lit. "days," may mean both 'days' and sg. 'year.'

[8] See comm. to 1:3.

[9] *Иоавонѣ* SU *Иоаву* АСК *Иову* В *Надву* D. ABCK emend *Иоавонъ to the more familiar biblical names Joab and Job. D contains the obviously corrupt *Иоаву* (*и > н*; *о > а*; *а > д*). SU (CS *Иоавонъ—Gk *Ἰοαβον) must preserve the primary form, apparently going back to the Heb combination with the theophoric prefix י(ו)- and און און means 'idolatry' in Hos 4:15; 5:8; 10:8, 15;12:12, Isa 41:29, 66:3; cf. also איש און Prov 6:12; Isa 55:7, בית און in Hos 4:15, במות און in Hos 9:8) or, less probably, עון 'wrong' (BDB:730b-731b; Jastrow 1903:1053). Heb און and עון may have been interchangeable in the rabbinic

The final *e* in SU (*Зоухе*), if it was not original (see below), may be treated as a result of ъ > *e* substitution in nom. sg. endings common in Novgorodian texts or, according to Uspenskij, reflecting the traditional pronunciation of literary Slavonic (Зализняк 1993:100–105; Успенский 1988). The form of instr. sg. *Зоухеемъ/Зоухиемъ* (nom. **Зоухии*) in 6:9 may be explained as the regular Slavic variation of short and full forms of personal names: *Зоухъ/Зоухии* (cf., e.g., CS *Дмитръ/Димитрии* from Gk Δημητριος, etc.; cf. Толкачев 1973). The name may go back to Semitic *zh* 'be proud,' *zwh* 'distrait, distracted,' *zhwh* 'haughty, high, mighty.' Cf. the name Azukhan in *2 En* (Vaillant 1952:122), probably derived from the same root: CS *Азоуханъ* < Gk *Αζουχαν < Aram *אזוחן (as causative אפע"ל form + suffix of substantivation – *ân* ?).

Greek magic papyri from Hellenistic period contain Ζεωχ as a god's name (Preisendanz 1928–1941:1.78,P.XII, 296), while the forms Ζουχ, Ζουκι (*ibid.*:1.130,P.IV,1919), Ζουχηλ (*ibid.*:2.65,P.XII,117) and twice Ζουχε (*ibid.*:1.132.P.IV,1983; 2.142,P.XIX,11) were identified by Preisendanz as "Zauberworte." Actually, they may be gods' names to the same extant as Ζεωχ brought above: Ζουχηλ has a theophoric suffix (-ηλ, Heb -אל) and the form Ζουχε is identical to CS *Зоухе* of the oldest versions of the *ApAb*. Moreover, in P.IV,1983 the name Zoukhe (Ζουχε) occurs in the prayer to Helios together with Iao (Ιαω, interchanged with the forms Ιαβω, Ιαβου, Ιαου; see *ibid.*:3.222–223),

---

period: cf. און גליון and עון גליון as derogatory equivalents for εὐαγγέλιον (*b.Shabbat* 110a). Gk magic papyri, besides other gods' names and "Zauberworte," contain similar Iavo, Iavu, Iau, Iao (Ιαβω, Ιαβου, Ιαου, Ιαω), supposed by Preisendanz to go back to Tetragrammaton (Preisendanz 1928–1941:3.222–223; Preisigke 1925–1941:3:39). On "Iao" used as a pagan god's name see Goodenough 1953–1968: 2.207, 245–258; Philonenko 1979.

[10] *что же Иоавонѣ бозѣ на друзѣмъ бозѣ* (*на друзѣмъ бозѣ* om. SU) *иже стоитъ съ Зухеемъ*. Bonw: "Was aber den Gott Joauv anlangt, welcher über den anderen Göttern mit Zucheus steht ...," BL: "the which is also the case with the god Joavon who standeth with Zucheus over the other gods...." These translations ignore the number of the second *бозѣ* and extraordinary use of the preposition *на*. Rub and RL translate literally: "Et quant à Ioavan, le dieu au-dessus de l'autre dieu qui se tient debout (avec) Souzouch ..."; "What about Ioav, the god on the other god, who stands with Zouchaios?" However, restoring the Gk *Vorlage* we reach an unambiguous interpretation: ὁ θεὸς ἐπὶ τῷ θεῷ ἄλλῳ "the god in power of another god," apparently a "minor god" (on the use of ἐπί in the sense of 'in the power of,' 'subordinated to' with dat., also in late and Byzantine sources; see LSJ:622; Sophocles:496). The translation of Gk ἐπί by its statistically most common CS counterpart *на*, stems either from translator's tendency to over-literal rendering or from his misunderstanding of the Greek phrase. This reading helps in the comprehension of the whole context: the golden Zoukh(e) is opposed to the major domestic god Mar-Umath made of stone (1:3), while the silver god Yoavon, *subordinated to the golden Zouch(e)*, is opposed to the minor domestic god Bar-Eshath made of wood (5:5).

while in *ApAb* the *golden* god Zoukh(e) (*Зоухе* of mss SU) stands beside the god named Yoavon (*Иоавонъ* of mss SU).

For more parallels from non-Jewish sources see 1:3 (on Mar Umath vs. Aram *mr ylhy* and Akk *mr byty*) and 5:5 (on Bar-Eshath vs. Ugaritic *yšt* and Phoenician (Greek) Φως, Πυρ, Φλοξ).

Conclusions

The classified collection of retroverted fragments presented in this work is intended to serve several purposes and to contribute to different fields of knowledge. Almost every retroverted reading may be further elaborated upon from the point of view of its contribution both to Jewish studies and to Slavic philology. We summarize below the possible applications of the materials presented in this study.

1. Apocalypse of Abraham

The primary goal of this work was to improve our understanding of the *Apocalypse of Abraham,* an extremely obscure text whose meaning can be explained only on the level of its Greek *Vorlage* and even its distant original. After retroversion, some fragments receive totally new meanings. Although we have generally refrained from seeking to carry this study beyond the purely philological goals set for it, our new understanding of the text, arrived at in keeping with these goals, has also clarified some issues that go well beyond philology *per se*. In particular, our study may be seen to shed light on such issues as the date and historical circumstances of the creation of *ApAb* (see 1:9; 9:9; also Kulik 1997b) as well as the milieu to which the original composition of the document is to be connected (see our *interpretatio judaica* for the supposedly Gnostic and Christian interpolations in comm. to 20:7; 29:3–13 and in the translation of 20:5 and 22:5). Below are listed some of the other notable items to emerge from our study that may have some bearing on the content of *ApAb*, items on which we hope to expand at greater length in the future.[1]

---

[1] *Theology*: (1) Verse 20:7 contains a noteworthy statement concerning the problem of the existence of evil in a monotheistic worldview: "Why then, if he [= Azazel] is not before [= aside] you [= God], have you set yourself with him?" The understanding of this question would help to clarify also the content of God's answer, which constitutes a significant part of the apocalypse. (2) The problem of theodicy is expressed by the following peculiar formula in 23:14: "you [= God] are angry at what was willed by you, at the one who does bad things according to your will/design [Gk βουλή]." (3) According to 26:5, freedom of will coexists with predetermination (cf. *Abot* 3,15): "As the will of your father [= sinful] is in him, as your will is in you [= righteous], so also the will desired by me [= God] is inevitable..." *Angelology*: (1) In 11:2 the angel Iahoel is described as appearing with the body of a griffon/eagle (like the angel Serapiel in *3 En* 26:3). (2) In 15:7 special angelic language is mentioned: "They [= the angels] were shouting in the language the words of which I did not know" (cf. *TestJob* 48:3; 49:2;

2. Jewish Pseudepigrapha

Besides the *Apocalypse of Abraham*, the literary tradition of the *Slavia Orthodoxa* preserved other valuable monuments of ancient religious thought. Such Slavonic texts as *2 Enoch* and the *Ladder of Jacob*, important versions of compositions preserved also in Greek such as *Apocalypse of Baruch (3 Baruch)*, *Testaments of the Twelve Patriarchs, Testament of Abraham, Life of Adam and Eve*, many fragments of *Palaea Interpretata,* etc., go back to the early pseudepigrapha and aggadic literature. The development of principles and tools for their retroversion is critical for understanding the information contained in the ancient sources, every bit of which is very valuable. This work is the first systematic attempt to apply retroversion to one such text, in order to solve its problems of interpretation. The material presented here is intended to make a contribution to the accumulation of such solutions and thus to pave the way to a developed general methodology of retroversion of Jewish pseudepigrapha preserved in Slavonic.

3. Church Slavonic literature

It is well known that "the main reason for incomprehensibility [of early Slavonic texts] is, of course, literal translation, and the list of works in which whole passages are completely without meaning in Slavonic is long ..." (Thomson 1978:117). In cases where the *Vorlage* has not survived, retroversion is the only way to deal with such a text. Understanding the literary production of the Slavs, especially in the "classic" period of Slavonic literature, irrespective of the significance of their *Vorlage,* is no less noble a scholarly task than the

---

50:1,2; 1 Cor 13:1). *History*: In 9:9 four main points of Jewish history are defined according to the destiny of the Temple: (1) building of the First Temple, (2) restoration of offerings by the righteous kings of the First Temple period, (3) building of the Second Temple, (4) renewed consecration (ἐγκαίνια, חנוכה) of the Second Temple. *Eschatology*: (1) 29:4–13 contains the Messiah (29:8–9) vs. anti-Messiah (29:4–8, 10–13) plot previously considered as an interpolated Christological description (cf. Licht (1971) and Hall (1988) on "Christian interpolations" in *ApAb*). (2) According to 28:3, in the last "hour" before the eschatological end Israel will live "in mercy and agreement" with the heathens. (3) Righteous men of the messianic world will feed on sacrifices like priests (29:18). *Exegesis*: In 23:10 Adam is defined as "reason" and Eve as "desire" (cf. Philo, *Leg. All.* II, 10, 14; *Quis Her.* 11). *Psychology*: In 6:3 the tripartite hierarchical nature of the soul is mentioned (cf. Philo, *Leg. Al.* I, 12–13 *et pass.*). *Liturgical practice*: In 1:2–3 "Terah's sacrificial services" are described following the order of the Second Temple daily morning *tamid* service according to *Tamid* 1–6; *Yoma* 2 (on the special place of the Temple, its service and priesthood in *ApAb* cf. *cosmology* 19:2–8 ("heavenly temple"), *history* 9:9, *eschatology* 29:18; cf. also 25:4).

investigation of their ancient originals. Our retroversion can also shed some light on the translation technique applied by the Slavs to Greek texts in the tenth to eleventh centuries.

4. Slavonic linguistics

Church Slavonic was created and developed as a language of translation from Greek. Studying translated texts with their extant *Vorlage* close at hand, or reconstructing their lost prototypes, is the only way to understand the function and development of Church Slavonic. The consequences of this phenomenon are noticeable also in later stages of the development of Slavic languages, up to the modern period. Retroversion allows us to improve our understanding of the linguistic phenomena found in Slavonic pseudepigrapha.[2]

---

[2] See, e.g., the following Slavonic *hapax legomena*: *измалъ* 'chisel' (1:8); *кокопилъ* 'Nile's grain' (?) (2:3); *настръзати* 'destroy' or *настръзати* 'carve' (1:1); *поновения* 'consecration' (9:9); *съпоношение* 'agreement' (28:5); *съпримиреныи* 'proportional' (6:9). Some well-known words occur in the document with unattested (or very rare) meanings, mainly as a result of calquing: *владыка* as 'domain' (30:6); *гласъ* as 'language' (15:7); *даръ* as 'sacrificial offering' (13:2); *изъглаголаемы* as 'explicit' (10:8); *купля* as 'affair, deal' (2:8); *ослаба* as 'willfulness' (29:8); *основати* as 'appoint' (26:1); *потъщати* as 'trouble' (27:12); *притещи* as 'descend' (27:3); *разграбити* as 'seize, take' (27:3,4); *срамитися* + dir. as 'reverence' (29:5); *свѣтъ* as 'fire' (5:8); *свѣтъ* as 'luminary' (9:3); *с(ъ)вѣтъ* as 'will,' 'reason' (22:2; 23:10; 23:14; 26:5–6; 29:10); *съходъ/съхода* as 'host,' 'gathering' (27:3; 28:4,5; see also other possibilities); *усѣчи* as 'hew' (1:9); *утврьдити* as 'sustain with food' (29:18). See also the examples

of irregular verb usage due to the syntactic structure of *Vorlage*: *гнѣватися* + dat. without prep. "be angry with" (23:14); *обладати въ* (27:11), *държати въ* (29:2), *властвовати въ* (31:2) as "rule over"; *срѣсти* + dat. "meet" (27:10); *творити власть* + *на* + acc. "have power over" (14:3); *тьзъ* + gen. "name-sake of" (10:3); *узрѣти въ* "see s.-th." (12:10; 31:4).

Abbreviations

The books of the Hebrew Bible and New Testament, Qumran documents, Rabbinic writings, apocrypha, pseudepigrapha, and Jewish Hellenistic writings are abbreviated according to the standard and well-known conventions. This applies equally to most of the (Old) Church Slavonic documents. MT, LXX, Aq, Sm, Th, NT are used to indicate, respectively, the Masoretic text, Septuagint, Aquila, Symmachus, Theodotion, and the New Testament. *GB* and *OB* designate, correspondingly, the Gennadij Bible of 1499 and the Ostrog Bible of 1581. All abbreviations are used without articles. For other abbreviations see *Manuscripts* and *References*.

A	*ApAb*, hypothetical Aramaic original
al.	*alii*, other mss.
Aram	Aramaic
Bulg	Bulgarian
CS	Church Slavonic
Ꙋ	*ApAb*, Greek *Vorlage*
Gk	Greek
ñ	*ApAb*, hypothetical Hebrew original
Heb	Hebrew
Lat	Latin
ms(s)	manuscript(s)
OCS	Old Church Slavonic
om.	omits
OR	Old Russian
Pol	Polish
Russ	Russian
S	*ApAb*, Church Slavonic prototext
SC	Serbo-Croatian
Slav	Slavic

Manuscripts

A Волоколамская толковая палея, М., РГБ, Моск. Дух. Акад. 172/549, XV в., 85–100; ed. Tikhonravov (54–78); descr. Яцимирский (1921:100).

B Синодальная толковая палея, М., ГИМ, 869 (Син. 211), XVI в., 76–90; ed. Rub (227–255); descr. *Описания* (1973:33).

C Толковая палея из собр. Московской Духовной Академии, М., РГБ, 173.III, #136, XVI в., 18–43.

D Историческая палея из собр. Тихонравова, М., РГБ, 299, № 704, XVI в., 145–175.

H М., РГБ, 242, № 100, XVI в., 145–175.

I Толковая палея из собр. Румянцева, М., РГБ, 256, № 361, XVI в., 94–114.

K Соловецкая палея, СПб., РНБ, Каз. Дух. Акад. 431, XVI-XVII вв., 79–92; ed. Porfir'ev (111–130).

O Толковая палея из собр. Вяземского, СПб., РНБ, 190, XVII в., 257–305.

S Сильвестровский сборник, М., ЦГАДА, Син. Тип. 53, XIV в., 164–183; ed. Срезневский (1861–1863:648–665); Tikhonravov (32–53); Новицкий (1891).

U Толковая иллюстрированная палея из собр. Уварова, М., ГИМ, собр. Уварова 85, XVI в., 299–313; descr. Леонид (Кавелин) (1894:3.9); Строев (1848:№ 286).

Later fragmentary and obviously secondary versions are not included.

References

References to the editions, translations, and commentaries to the *Apocalypse of Abraham* give the verse under discussion without noting the page.

Barr, James. *Comparative Philology and the Text of Old Testament*. Oxford: Clarendon Press, 1968.
BDB = Brown Francis B., Samuel R. Driver, and Charles A. Briggs. *The New Brown-Driver-Briggs-Gesenius Hebrew-English Lexicon*. Boston, New York: Houghton Mifflin, 1906.
Ben-Yehuda, Eliezer. *Thesaurus Totius Hebraitatis et veteris et recentioris* [Hebrew]. Jerusalem: Ben-Yehuda, 1948–1959.
БК = Борковский, Виктор Иванович, Петр Саввич Кузнецов. *Историческая грамматика русского языка*. Москва: "Наука", 1965.
BL = Box, George H., and Joseph I. Landsman. *The Apocalypse of Abraham*. London: Society for Promoting Christian Knowledge, 1918.
Bonw = Bonwetsch, Gottlieb Nathanael. *Die Apocalypse Abrahams* (= Studien zur Geschichte der Theologie und der Kirche. Bd.1, Heft 1). Leipzig: A. Deichert, 1897.
Charlesworth, James H. *The Old Testament Pseudepigrapha*. Garden City, N.Y.: Doubleday, 1983-1985.
Dal' = Даль, Владимир Иванович. *Толковый словарь живого великорусского языка*. Москва: Общество любителей российской словесности, 1863–1866.
DDD = Van der Toorn, Karel, Bob Becking and Pieter W. van der Horst (eds.). *Dictionary of Deities and Demons in the Bible*. Leiden, Boston: Brill; Grand Rapids, Mich.: Eerdmans, 1999.
Dean-Otting, Mary. "The Apocalypse of Abraham." Idem. *Heavenly Journeys: A Study of the Motif in Hellenistic Jewish Literature*. Frankfurt am Main, Bern, New York: P. Lang, 1984: 248–261.
Dietrich, Manfred, Oswald Loretz, and Joaquín Sanmartín. "Die keil-alphabethische Texte aus Ugarit." *Alter Orient und Altes Testament* 24 (1976).
Dostál, Antonin. *Studie o vidovém systému v staroslověnštině*. Praha: Státní pedagogické nakl., 1954.
Dvoretskij = Дворецкий, Иосиф Хананович. *Древнегреческо-русский словарь*. Москва: Гос. изд-во иностранных и национальных словарей, 1958.

Filin = Филин, Федот Петрович, *et al. Словарь русских народных говоров.* Ленинград: "Наука", 1965-.

Франко, Иван. «Крехівська Палея». Idem. *Пам'яткі українсько-руської мови і літератури.* Т. 1. Львів: Т-во им. Т. Шевченка, 1896.

Frey, Jean Baptiste. "Abraham (Apocalypse d')." *Dictionnaire de la Bible.* Supplément. V. 1. Paris: Letouzey et Ané, 1928-1966.

Genizah-Fragmente = Schäfer, Peter (ed.). *Genizah-Fragmente zur Heikhalot-Literatur.* Tübingen: Mohr, 1984.

Ginzberg, Louis. "Abraham, Apocalypse of." *The Jewish Encyclopedia.* V. 1. New York, London: Funk and Wagnalls, 1901-06: 91–92.

Ginzberg, Louis. *The Legends of the Jews.* Philadelphia: Jewish publication society of America, 1909–1938.

Goodenough, Erwin R. *Jewish Symbols in the Greco-Roman Period.* [New York:] Pantheon Books, 1953–1968.

Green, Tamara M. *The City of the Moon God. Religious Traditions of Harran.* Leiden, New York: Brill, 1992.

Hall, Robert H. "The Christian Interpolation in the Apocalypse of Abraham." *Journal of Biblical Literature* 107/1 (1988): 107–112.

Horovitz, Chaim Meir. *Agudat agadot: kovets midrashim ketanim* [Hebrew]. Berlin, 1881.

HR = Hatch, Edwin, and Henry A. Redpath. *A Concordance to the Septuagint and other Greek Versions of the Old Testament.* Grand Rapids, Mich.: Baker Books Graz, 1998.

Istrin = Истрин, Василий Михайлович. *Замечания о составе Толковой палеи* (= *Сборник отделения русского языка и словестности Императорской академии наук.* Т. 65, No. 6). С.-Петербург: Тип. Имп. академии наук, 1898.

Istrin 1920–1922 = Истрин, Василий Михайлович. *Хроника Георгия Амартола.* Петроград: Российская гос. акад. тип., 1920–1930.

Jastrow, Markus. *Dictionary of the Targumim, the Talmud Babli and Yerushalmi, and the Midrashic Literature.* London: Luzac & Co.; New York: G. P. Putnam's sons, 1903.

Jellinek, Adolf. *Bet Ha-Midrash.* Leipzig: C.W. Vollrath, 1853–1878.

Яцимирский, Александр Иванович. *Библиографический обзор апокрифов в южнославянской и русской письменности (Списки памятников),* вып. 1: *Апокрифы ветхозаветные.* Петроград: Отделение русского языка и словесности Российской академии наук, 1921.

Копыленко, М. М. «Кальки греческого происхождения в языке древнерусской письменности». *Византийский временник* 34 (1973): 141–150.

Kulik 1997a = Кулик, Александр. «Об одном церковнославянском гапаксе». *Palaeoslavica* 5 (1997): 339–345.

Kulik 1997b = Кулик, Александр. «К датировке Откровения Авраама». *In Memoriam: Памяти Я. С. Лурье.* С.-Петербуог, 1997: 189–195.

Kulik 2002 = Кулик, Александр. «Откровение Авраама». *Вестник Еврейского университета* 5 (2002): 231-254.
Kutscher, Edward Yechezkel. *A History of the Hebrew Language*. Jerusalem: Magnes Press, 1982.
Lampe = Lampe, Geoffrey W. H. *A Patristic Greek Lexicon*. Oxford, New York: Clarendon Press, 1961.
Lee, John A. L. *A Lexical Study of the Septuagint Version of the Pentateuch*. Chico, CA: Scholars Press, 1983.
Леонид, архимандрит (Кавелин, Лев Александрович). *Систематическое описание славяно-российских рукописей собрания графа А. С. Уварова*. Москва: Тип. А. И. Мамонтова, 1894.
Licht, Jacob. "Abraham, Apocalypse of," *Encyclopaedia Judaica*. V. 2. Jerusalem: Encyclopaedia Judaica, 1971-1978: 125–127.
Lunt, Horace G. "On the Language of the Slavonic Apocalypse of Abraham." *Slavica Hierosolymitana* 7 (1985): 55–62.
LSJ = Liddell, Henry G., Robert Scott, and Henry S. Jones. *A Greek-English Lexicon (with a Revised Supplement)*. Oxford: Clarendon Press, 1996.
Margulies, Mordecai. *Midrash hagadol on the Pentateuch, Genesis* [Hebrew]. Jerusalem: Mosad Harav Kook, 1947.
Meillet, Antoine. *Études sur l'étymologie et le vocabulaire du vieux slave*. V. 2. Paris: Bouillon, 1905.
Meillet, Antoine. *Le Slave Commun*. Paris: H. Champion, 1934.
Mikl = Miklosich, Franz, Ritter von. *Lexicon Palaeoslovenico-Graeco-Latinum*. Vindobonae: G. Braumüller, 1862–1865.
Milik, Josef T. "Milkî-sedeq et Milkî-reša dans les ancients écrits juifs et chrétiens." *Journal of Jewish Studies* 23 (1972): 95–144.
Molnár, Nándor. *The Calques of Greek Origin in the Most Ancient Old Slavic Gospel Texts* (= *Slavistische Vorschungen* 17). Budapest: Akademiai Kiad, 1985.
Moulton, James H., and George Milligan. *The Vocabulary of the Greek Testament*. London: Hodder and Stoughton, 1930.
Muraoka, Takamitsu. *Hebrew/Aramaic Index to the Septuagint*. Grand Rapids, Mich.: Baker Books, 1998.
Nida, Eugene Albert. *Towards a Science of Translating with Special Reference to Principles and Procedures Involved in Bible Translation*. Leiden: Brill, 1964.
Новицкий, П. П. (ed.). *Откровение Авраама* (= *Общество любителей древней письменности*. Т. 99, No. 2). С.-Петербург: Тип. А. Ф. Маркова, 1891 (facsimile edition).
Odeberg, Hugo. *3 Enoch: or the Hebrew Book of Enoch*. Cambridge: University Press, 1928.
Olofsson, Staffan. *The LXX version: A Guide to the Translation Technique of the Septuagint*. Stockholm: Almqvist & Wiksell, 1990.

Описания = Протасева, Татьяна Николаевна. *Описания рукописей Синодального собрания, не вошедших в описание А В. Горского и К. И. Невоструева*. Ч. 2. Москва, 1973.

Otrębski, Jan Szczepan. "Pochodzenie tzw. Boudouinowskiej palatalizacji w językach słowiańskich." *Slavia Occidentalis* 19 (1948): 23–62.

Pennington = Pennington, A. "The Apocalypse of Abraham," Sparks, Hedley F. D. (ed.). *The Apocryphal Old Testament*. Oxford: Clarendon Press, 1985: 363–392.

Phil = Philonenko-Sayar, Belkis, and Marc Philonenko. *L'Apocalypse d'Abraham* (= *Semitica* 31). Paris: Librairie d'Amérique et d'Orient Adrien-Maisonneuve, 1981.

Philonenko, Marc. "L'Anguipède alectorocéphale et le dieu Iaô." *Académie des Inscriptions & Belles-Lettres* (1979): 297–304.

Porfir'ev = Порфирьев, Иван Яковлевич. «Откровение Авраама». Idem, *Апокрифические сказания о ветхозаветных лицах и событиях* (= *Сборник отделения русского языка и словестности Императорской академии наук* 17.1). С.-Петербург: Тип. Имп. академии наук, 1877: 111–130.

Preisendanz, Karl, et al. *Papyri Graecae Magicae*. Leipzig, Berlin: B.G. Teubner, 1928–1941.

Preisigke, Friedrich. *Wörterbuch der Griekischen Papyrusurkunden*. Berlin: Selbstverlag der Erben, 1925–1931.

Пыпин, Александр Николаевич. *Ложные и отреченные книги славянской и русской старины* (= *Памятники старинной русской литературы, издаваемые Графом Григорием Кушелевым-Безбородко*. Т. 3). С.-Петербург: Тип. П. А. Кулеша, 1860-62.

Riessler, Paul. "Apocalypse Abrahams." Riessler, Paul. *Altjüdisches Schrifttum ausserhalb der Bibel*. Augsburg: B. Filser, 1928: 13–39.

RL = "The Apocalypse of Abraham. Translated by R. Rubinkiewicz. Revised and noted by H. G. Lunt." Charlesworth, James H. *The Old Testament Pseudepigrapha*. Garden City, N.Y.: Doubleday, 1983-1985. V. 2: 689–705.

Rub = Rubinkiewicz, Ryszard. *L'Apocalypse d'Abraham en vieux slave*. Lublin: Société des Lettres et des Sciences de l'Université Catholique de Lublin, 1987.

Rubinkiewicz, Ryszard. "Apokalipsa Abraham." *Ruch Biblijny i Liturgiczny* 27 (1974): 230–237.

Rubinkiewicz, Ryszard. "La vision de l'histoire dans l'Apocalypse d'Abraham." *Aufstieg und Niedergang der romischen Welt*. B. II, 19, 1. Berlin, New York: W. de Gruyter, 1979: 137–151.

Rubinkiewicz, Ryszard. "Les Semitismes dans L'Apocalypse d'Abraham." *Folia Orientalia* 21 (1980): 141–148.

Rubinstein, Arie. "Hebraisms in the Slavonic Apocalypse of Abraham." *Journal of Jewish Studies* 4 (1953): 108–115.

Rubinstein, Arie. "Hebraisms in the Slavonic Apocalypse of Abraham." *Journal of Jewish Studies* 5 (1954): 132–135.
Rubinstein, Arie. "A Problematic Passage in the Apocalypse of Abraham." *Journal of Jewish Studies* 8 (1957): 45–50.
Schäfer, Peter, *et al. Synopse zur Heikhalot-Literatur.* Tübingen: Mohr, 1981.
Schäfer, Peter, *et al. Konkordanz zur Heikhalot-Literatur.* Tübingen: Mohr, 1986–1988.
Schleusner, Johann Friedrich. *Novum Lexicon Graeco-Latinum im Novum Testamentum.* Glasgow: A. et J. M. Duncan, 1817.
Scholem, Gershom Gerhard. *Major Trends in Jewish Mysticism.* New York: Schocken Books, 1946 (1st ed. 1941).
Schumann, Kurt. *Die griechischen Lehnbildungen und Lehnbedeutungen im Altbulgarischen.* Wiesbaden: O. Harrassowitz, 1958.
Schürer, Emil (revised by Vermes, Geza, and Fergus Millar), *The History of the Jewish People in the Age of Jesus Christ.* Edinburgh: Clark, 1973.
SDRJa11–14 = Аванесов, Рубен Иванович, *et al. Словарь древнерусского языка* (XI-XIV вв.). Москва: "Русский язык", 1988-.
Shevelov, George Yuri. *A Prehistory of Slavic: the Historical Phonology of Common Slavic.* Heidelberg: C. Winter, 1964.
Slov = Kurz, Josef, *et al. Slovnik Jazyka Staroslovenskego.* Praha: Nakl. Ceskosl. akademie, 1958- .
Sokoloff, Michael. *A Dictionary of Jewish Palestinian Aramaic of the Byzantine Period.* Ramat-Gan: Bar Ilan University Press, 1990.
Sophocles = Sophocles, Evangelinus Apostolides. *A Glossary of Later and Byzantine Greek,* Cambridge, Boston: Welch, Bigelow & Co, 1860.
Srezn = Срезневский, Измаил Иванович. *Материалы для словаря древнерусского языка по письменным памятникам.* С.-Петербург: Тип. Имп. академии наук, 1893–1903.
Срезневский, Измаил Иванович. *Сказания о святых Борисе и Глебе. Сильвестровский список XIV века.* С.-Петербург: Тип. Имп. академии наук, 1860.
Срезневский, Измаил Иванович. «Книги Откровения Авраме». *Известия Императорской академии наук по отделению русского языка и словестности.* Т. 10. С.-Петербург: Тип. Имп. Академии наук, 1861–1863, 648–665.
SRJa11–17 = *Словарь русского языка XI–XVII вв.* Москва: "Наука", 1975–.
Строев, Павел Михайлович. *Рукописи славянския и российския принадлежащия... И. Н. Царскому.* Москва: Тип. Готье, 1848.
Thackeray. Henry St. J. *A Grammar of the Old Testament in Greek.* Cambridge: University Press, 1909.
Thomson, Francis J. "The Nature of the Reception of Christian Byzantine Culture in Russia in the Tenth to Thirteenth Centuries and Its Implications to Russian Culture." *Slavica Gandensia* 5 (1978): 107–139.

Thomson 1988a = Thomson, Francis J. "Towards a Typology of Errors in Slavonic Translations." Farrugia, Edward G., Robert F. Taft, and Gino K. Piovesana (eds.). *Christianity among the Slavs: The Heritage of Saint Cyril and Methodius* (= *Orientalia Christiana Analecta*, 231). Roma: Pont. Institutum Studiorum Orientalium, 1988: 351–380.

Thomson 1988b = Thomson, Francis J. "Sensus or Proprietas Verborum. Medieval Theories of Translation from Greek into Latin and Slavonic." *Selecta Slavica* 13 (1988): 675–691.

Tikhonravov = Тихонравов, Николай Саввич. «Откровение Авраама». idem. *Памятники отреченной русской литературы.* С.-Петербург: "Общественная польза", 1863. Т. 1: 32–78.

Толкачев, А. И. «Основные факторы фонетических изменений в заимствованных греко-христианских именах в древнерусском языке». *VII международный съезд славистов: доклады советской делегации.* Москва, 1973: 252–271.

Tov, Emanuel. *The Text-Critical Use of the Septuagint in Biblical Research.* Jerusalem: Simor, 1997.

Трубачев, Олег Николаевич, *et al. Этимологический словарь славянских языков.* Москва: "Наука", 1974-.

Troubetzkoy, N. "Essai sur la chronologie de certains faits phonétiques du slave commun." *Revue des études slaves* 2 (1922): 217–234.

Turdeanu, Emil. "L'Apocalypse d'Abraham en slave." *Journal for the Study of Judaism* 3 (1972): 153–180 (repr.: Turdeanu, Emil. *Apocryphes slaves et roumains de l'Ancien Testament.* Leiden: Brill, 1981: 173–200).

Успенский, Борис Андреевич. «Русское книжное произношение XI–XII вв. и его связь с южнославянской традицией (чтение еров)». *Актуальные проблемы славянского языкознания.* Москва: Изд-во МГУ, 1988: 99–156.

Vaillant, André. *Le Livre des Secrets d'Hénoch.* Paris: Institut d'études slaves, 1952.

Vaillant, André. *Grammaire Comparée des Langues Slaves.* Paris: Institut d'études slaves, 1966.

Vasmer = Фасмер, Макс (с доп. О. Н. Трубачева, под ред. Б. А. Ларина). *Этимологический словарь русского языка.* Москва: "Прогресс", 1986–87.

Vondrák, Václav., "O pozdějších palatalisacích v praslavanštině." *Slavia* 2 (1923/24): 17–25.

Востоков Александр Христофорович. *Описание русских и словенских рукописей Румянцевскаго музеума.* С.-Петербург: Тип. Имп. Академии наук, 1842.

Wasserstrom, Steven M., "Jewish Pseudepigrapha and Qiṣaṣ al-Anbiyā'." Hary, Benjamin H., John L. Hayes, and Fred Astren Hary (eds.). *Judaism and Islam: Boundaries, Communications and Interaction (Essays in Honor of William M. Brinner).* Leiden, Boston, Köln: Brill, 2000: 237–256.

Weitzman, Steven. "The Song of Abraham." *Hebrew Union College Annual* 65 (1994): 21–33.
Wohlberg, Robert. *Grundlinien einer talmudischen Psychologie*. Berlin: E. Wertheim, 1902.
Зализняк, Андрей Анатольевич. "Лингвистические исследования и словоуказатель." Янин, Валентин Лаврентьевич, Андрей Анатольевич Зализняк. *Новогородские грамоты на бересте (из раскопок 1984–1989 гг.)*. Москва: "Наука", 1993: 191–343.

www.ingramcontent.com/pod-product-compliance
Lightning Source LLC
Chambersburg PA
CBHW031321150426
43191CB00005B/279